# Creative Computer Crafts!

D1280591

2173718
6/06

**Creative Computer Crafts.** Copyright ©2006 by Marcelle Costanza

All rights reserved. No part of this work may be reproduced or transmitted in any form or by any means, electronic or mechanical, including photocopying, recording, or by any information storage or retrieval system, without the prior written permission of the copyright owner and the publisher.

Printed in China

Trademarked names are used throughout this book. Rather than use a trademark symbol with every occurrence of a trademarked name, we are using the names only in an editorial fashion and to the benefit of the trademark owner, with no intention of infringement of the trademark.

PUBLISHER: William Pollock
MANAGING EDITOR: Elizabeth Campbell
COVER AND INTERIOR DESIGN AND COMPOSITION: Red Light Design
COPYEDITOR: Sarah Lemaire
PROOFREADER: Nancy Riddiough

For information on translations or book distributors outside the United States and Canada, please contact No Starch Press, Inc. directly:

No Starch Press, Inc.
555 De Haro Street, Suite 250, San Francisco, CA 94107
phone: 415.863.9900; fax 415.863.9950; info@nostarch.com; http://www.nostarch.com

The information in this book is distributed on an "As Is" basis, without warranty. While every precaution has been taken in the preparation of this work, neither the author nor No Starch Press, Inc. shall have any liability to any person or entity with respect to any loss or damage caused or alleged to be caused directly or indirectly by the information contained in it.

Library of Congress Cataloguing-in-Publication Data

Costanza, Marcelle.
  Creative computer crafts : 50 fun and useful projects you can make with any inkjet printer / Marcelle Costanza.
    p. cm.
 ISBN 1-59327-068-2
 1. Computer art. 2. Handicraft. I. Title.
 TT869.5.C67 2005
 745.5--dc22
                                      2005024813

# Creative Computer Crafts!

50 fun and useful projects you can make with any inkjet printer

by Marcelle Costanza

**NO STARCH PRESS**

In Memory of my dear friend **Shelley Woods**
She always told me one thing — *"You go, girl!"*
I did it, Shelley!

This book is dedicated to my husband, Chris, who put up with several months of my disappearing to my basement office for days at a time in order to create this book. I love you, honey.

## Acknowledgments

I would like to extend my sincere thanks to the crew at No Starch Press for deciding to publish a second book on computer crafting. It takes a wise team to realize that this crafting genre is growing and that computers have other uses besides word processing, spread sheets, playing games and surfing the Internet.

In particular I wish to thank Bill Pollock for his insight and his incredible patience. My gratitude also extends to Susan Berge and Elizabeth Campbell for their production skills, Jim Compton and Sarah Lemaire for their patience in editing, Leigh Poehler for her marketing expertise and Red Light Design for the layout and cover design.

Others who deserve my thanks include my Mom and Dad and my siblings for their constant encouragement, particularly my mother, who has been bugging me to write a book since I penned my first short story at age 7.

And again, my thanks to my husband Chris, who put up with months of my panic attacks over getting this project completed.

# Contents

**PART 2  45**

**Projects**

**Appendix A: Computer Crafting Websites and Message Boards  140**

**Appendix B: Resources: Where to Find Hardware, Software, and Computer Crafting Supplies  142**

**Appendix C: Templates  145**

**Index  157**

# Introduction

I've been a crafter since the early 1980s, before I had ever touched a computer. It was not until I took a job in 1986 that I had my "own" computer in my office, a DOS-based system with a monochrome monitor and a big, noisy dot matrix printer. One of the physicians I worked with gave me a print program and I soon discovered that I could print images on the pin-feed paper on that old printer – images that were comprised of bunches of black and white characters. I made a banner for an office party and shortly after that other employees were asking for custom printed items.

Little did I know that this innocently learned skill would turn into my own business and a downright obsession. It began when I bought my first computer in 1995 and began designing our family Christmas cards. That led to searching the Internet for any collection of clipart I could get my hands on. I soon discovered there was a small, slowly growing group of folks out there who were as tickled as I that the computer could be used for such creative endeavors. I began to purchase specialty inkjet papers and tried my hand at different projects. And the more I tried the more I wanted to create. I began to go to bed at night literally dreaming up new projects. Some nights I would get out of bed and head to my computer because I just had to try out an idea or I would never be able to sleep. I saw the sun rise on many of those occasions.

When I decided to try my hand at running my own computer crafting business, the most important thing to me was being able to share some of my project ideas with other people. So I started a website that offered a few specialty inkjet items and decided to post all the projects I had made and include the instructions for each of them–free to whomever wanted them. Those first dozen or so projects have now blossomed into over 70 and some of the visitors to my website have even been gracious enough to let me post some of their own creations. Then came the Crafter's Gallery, and the mailing list, and the message board, and the now annual Computer Crafting Contest.

And finally came this book. I decided I had to create some new projects for it; projects that aren't available on my website. So in addition to working on the manuscript and taking all the photos and creating all the screen shots and diagrams, I designed a couple of new projects specifically for the book.

I have thoroughly enjoyed writing this book. I hope you will enjoy it as well. If you have any questions or comments, I'd love to hear from you! You can email me at computercrafts@patmedia.net. You can also visit my website at www.thecraftypc.com.

CHAPTER ONE

# The Road to Computer Crafting

# The Road to Computer Crafting

*As a road map to your exploration of computer crafting—using your personal computer, printer, digital camera or scanner, and craft software to create all or part of a craft project—this chapter first describes my own evolution as a computer crafter and the increasing popularity of crafts in general. You'll learn some of the benefits, inside and outside the classroom, of computer crafting.*

## The Evolution of Computer Crafting

When I started crafting 25 years ago, the market was a totally different animal than it is now. In my neighborhood in New York City there were only two craft stores, and they were minuscule. Their inventories were composed mainly of fabrics, wooden boxes, and various embellishments—acrylic craft paints, lace, and beading by the yard—a far cry from the myriad of items you can find in today's craft superstores and on the Internet.

My first crafting "tool" was a hot glue gun, and no one else I knew had one. Due to the lack of materials available back then, my crafting was composed primarily of fabric and lace-covered photo albums, placemats with ribbon and lace embellishments (there was no such thing as wired ribbon back then!), and hanging candle holders made from wooden embroidery hoops, wooden candle cups, and that ever-present lace and ribbon.

Then I came across plaster crafts and began frequenting the only source of plaster figurines in my area. My apartment was immediately overrun by a farm of plaster creatures, all waiting to be colored and given personality with nothing more than a paintbrush and some acrylic craft paints. I remember staying up well past midnight just to put the finishing touches on a pair of plaster seahorses or a plaster picture frame I would give as a gift. I started to sell the finished pieces at local craft fairs and flea markets, and the marvelous response from the customers made me realize that something I

loved doing could actually pay off.

A few of those crafting projects and I was hooked. Next, I tried my hand at stenciling, but since precut stencils were hard to find and since I did not own a computer back then, I drew and cut out my own stencils and applied them using acrylic craft paints and cosmetic sponge wedges. My taste for crafting increased with every new project I tried, and I was aching for a source of new materials.

A trip to visit my family in Virginia in the late 1980s proved to be the start of the career that resulted in this book. There I was introduced to the first craft superstore I had ever seen. I walked into this place—large even by today's standards—and I became that proverbial kid in the candy store. I strolled down each and every aisle, trying to take it all in, practically drooling at the selection of craft materials. Needless to say, my wallet was empty by the time I left that store.

Shortly after that trip, one of those craft superstores opened not far from where I lived, and I was there almost every weekend. I've always had a love of paper— in every color, shape, and size—so I suppose I was destined to wind up a computer crafting addict. Scrapbooking was in its infancy at that time, and even though I had never tried my hand at that particular craft, the assortment of papers available in that local craft superstore made me giddy. Not sure what I would actually use them for, I began stocking up on all sorts of neat and unusual papers—and I suppose the rest is history.

## Computers Enter the Picture

I did not purchase my first computer until I moved out of New York in 1995—there was simply no room for one in my tiny apartment. My only experience with computers prior to that move had been on a job I held as a medical administrator in Manhattan. The Windows operating system was in its infancy at that time, although the Macintosh operating system with its GUI (graphical user interface) was as alive and well as it is today. The PC I worked on was DOS-based, and the only affordable printers around in the mid-1980s were dot matrix printers—you know, the kind they use down at the garage to print your car repair bill. But that's when I got my first taste of computer crafting. I discovered print programs that let me make banners, cards, and other nifty things. Soon, many of my co-workers were asking for specially designed items.

So I made that move to New Jersey and bought my first PC, a color inkjet printer, and a program called PrintMaster, and that was it. Once I discovered what I could do with that program and an inkjet printer, my poor husband could not pry me away from that machine.

My next technology purchase was a scanner. I began to learn how to scan and edit photos, and soon I was making our holiday cards, which sported photos of my spouse that were so hysterical, the friends and family who received them would call or write just to say what a kick they got out of them. That was 10 years ago, and that Christmas card tradition still stands. My husband has been the main character of every card since that first card, and they have become more elaborate every year. I had one aunt who kept every single one of them on her mantle year in and year out. See Figure 1-1 for an example.

A few years and a few newer computers later, I decided in 1999 that I wanted to do this for a living. Now I work as a graphic designer and have my own business in—what else—computer crafts! In the spring of 2000, my business was born, and I have loved every single minute of it. The crafting industry itself has grown in leaps and bounds in that time. Craft superstores like Michael's, The Rag Shop, Hobby Lobby, and A.C. Moore

**Figure 1-1:** One of our recent Christmas cards

The inside of the same card

to mention a few, are springing up in every community. National craft shows are touring all over the country, and even television has gotten into the act with numerous programs geared toward the crafter—quilting, scrap-booking, jewelry making, greeting card programs, and the best of them all in my opinion—the Carol Duvall Show.

At the same time that personal computers and printers were becoming more powerful and cheaper and the crafting hobby was exploding in popularity, another revolution was taking place: digital photography. Millions of people can now capture their own images to use in craft projects. Digital photography makes it simpler to edit, do some fancy cropping or adjust color and brightness right on your computer screen.

Computer crafting has come into its own in the last few years. Just take a look on the Internet at the ever-increasing number of computer crafting websites, forums, and bulletin boards. They're everywhere! Even Carol Duvall has added many computer crafting projects to her program. I've manned something of a one-woman crusade with some of the crafting associations to which I belong to make certain that computer crafting gets the recognition it deserves.

## The Benefits of Crafting

In 2001, an organization called HIA (Hobby Industry of America—now known as the Craft and Hobby Association, CHA, since it merged with ACCI, the Association of Crafts and Creative Industries) published a study on the benefits of crafting in schools. Those of us who have been crafting for years already know these benefits include reduced stress, increased imagination and creativity, increased self-esteem, and general feelings of accomplishment; but it was reassuring to see it studied by such a prestigious crafting organization, especially in the area of education. The key points of this study are as follows:

• A significant number of teachers use hands-on projects to advance learning. Teachers regularly use hands-on craft projects to teach the core subjects.

• Student learning improves when classroom lessons incorporate hands-on craft projects. Teachers say hands-on projects enhance the instructional process and help students learn both basic information and more complex ideas.

• Students who spend a greater proportion of their classroom learning time engaged in hands-on projects score significantly higher on writing and drawing knowledge application tasks.

• The use of crafts for learning increases the students' creativity and level of detail.

• Students develop greater curiosity about the subject matter when hands-on craft projects are included.

•Teachers say learning through hands-on craft projects accommodates students with different learning styles.

• Student behavior and socialization skills improve when hands-on craft projects are undertaken.

It is clear from this report that general arts and crafts, used in conjunction with more traditional educational tools, benefit our children.

Just think what they could learn if computer crafting were added to the mix! With the steady stream of technological advances being made in all areas of computing, computer crafting stands to give our kids a leg up on the competition by teaching them necessary computer skills while making it fun in the process!

Your children are not the only ones who benefit from crafting. Crafting provides you with a tool that allows for social interaction, helps you to maintain mental acuity and manual dexterity, and keeps your imagination honed. And as adults, you also need to keep up your computer skills!

## Computer Crafting on the World Wide Web

The number of sites on the Web related to computer crafting is growing by leaps and bounds. Not only is there a wealth of websites providing free computer crafting projects and the supplies necessary to complete those projects, but there's also an increasing number of "How To" sites that explain the basics of using your computer as an artistic tool. With this plethora of knowledge as close as your computer screen, there is no reason why anyone with a computer and a love of crafting cannot become a pro at computer crafting. I've had folks contact me desperate for help and convinced they could never learn computer crafting. With just a short "You can do it" pep talk and a few step-by-step instructions to get them started, they are well on their way.

For example, recently I was contacted by a woman in Tennessee in a panic because she needed to create some items for an award program for her son. She was convinced she didn't have the necessary computer skills to get it done. I walked her through the process, even doing one or two of the pieces for her, and in a matter of days she had completed the entire project on her own. Not only was her son elated, but she is now getting requests from friends and neighbors for her computer crafting handiwork!

The Web has become a virtual treasure trove of free computer craft projects and message boards filled with folks captivated with this crafting genre who are anxious to share ideas and knowledge. The best of those sites and forums are listed in Appendix A, "Computer Crafting Websites and Message Boards," at the back of this book.

## Creativity and Today's Technology

How many people would consider a computer as a tool for crafting? Not as many as you might think. For the majority of the population, a home PC is used primarily for surfing, gaming, word processing, bill paying, business tasks, etc. Of course, graphic artists use their computers for photo editing, graphic designers use them for logos and other artwork, and website designers and computer animators do some truly amazing things with computers. But crafting is not considered a task normally associated with computers.

Well, that's changing! With the advent of programs that allow you to make greeting cards or create scrapbook pages or even needlepoint patterns, the field of computer crafting is exploding. Take the aforementioned program PrintMaster, for example. I have been using this program since version 3. I began using it about 10 years ago, and at that time, you could do greeting cards, posters, banners, labels, business cards, and a few other projects. PrintMaster is now up to version 16, and it includes an entire section devoted to crafts—everything from general crafts to "Fun for Kids," "Homework Helpers," "Kitchen Crafts," and "Party Goods."

PrintMaster is not the only program that has realized that folks are more and more interested in creating crafts using their computers. Print Shop and Print Artist are other programs that have added crafts to their repertoire.

As far as photo editing, with the right program and a bit of practice you can do some pretty amazing things with your computer. Just take a look at the before and after photos in Figures 1-2 and 1-3 to get an idea of what you can do with your PC!

This isn't all you can do with photo editing. We did custom invitations for an anniversary party that included a black-and-white wedding photo. The family of the couple wanted some color in the photo, so we added color just to sections of the photo—a pale pink on the bride's satin shoes and some pink in her bouquet and on her lips—as you can see in Figure 1-4.

You don't need to be an expert in programs like Photoshop (the tool I used for the disappearing act and color touchup) to do fancy editing on photos. PrintMaster and most other graphics program titles include a photo editor that allows you to adjust colors or take color out all together. You can adjust brightness and contrast, crop photos into fancy shapes, and even apply some impressive filters that can turn your photos into works of art with just a few clicks of a mouse. Add those edited photos to some of your computer crafts for a truly personalized project. Computers are a true crafting tool!

## Growth of the Computer Crafting Field

There's no doubt that crafting in general has become a multi-billion-dollar business. Just visit any of your larger craft store like Michael's, Hobby Lobby, A.C. Moore, and the like, and you'll never find the places lacking customers. In 2002 alone, $29.0 billion—yes *billion*—was spent on crafting. While the majority of those dollars were spent on crafting genres that don't involve computing, there is evidence that this segment of the crafting industry is growing as well. This is apparent when you realize that more and more crafting software and books related to computer crafts are becoming

available to consumers. Just type the phrase "arts and crafts software" into a search engine, and it results in over two million hits!

As explained in the previous section, the number of websites and message boards devoted to computer crafting has also grown tremendously in just the last few years. Five years ago you were lucky if you could find two or three websites or message boards. Now they are everywhere on the Web. The variety of sites and boards now available is astonishing.

Sadly, the major arts and crafts organizations in this country are slow to recognize the impact of this type of crafting on the industry as a whole. Hopefully, this will change in the very near future, since computer crafting is not only a viable and growing field, but has the added benefit of providing a fun way to learn computer skills, not only for adults but also for children. The report mentioned in the previous section already shows that crafting provides for improved learning when classroom lessons incorporate hands-on craft projects. It stands to reason that this can also translate into improved computer skills if those hands-on craft projects include the use of a computer as a crafting tool.

**Figure 1-2:** This is the original photo. The bride wanted it edited to remove herself from the picture so she could give her husband a photo of his parents together.

**Figure 1-3:** After some editing in Photoshop, the bride now has a photo of her in-laws alone!

**Figure 1-4:** An example of a photograph with some sections colorized

## Computer Crafting in the Classroom:
### *Teaching Computer Skills with Computer Crafting*

Anyone with young children and a computer in the house knows that their little ones are learning computer skills faster than they are! This is due in part to their natural curiosity. Children are like sponges—they soak up information at a rate far exceeding their adult counterparts. And in a world that is increasingly based on ever-changing technology, computer skills are essential for your children if they are to survive and prosper in the future.

Many schools now have computer labs and consider computer skills a critical part of their curriculum. Some children, however, may be intimidated by this technology, particularly if they do not have a computer in their home. Teaching the basics of computer skills is the easy part. Getting kids to love this learning is another

story. That's where computer crafting comes into play. A child who can learn a skill and come away with something tangible that they created will be more eager to continue that learning.

Crafting in schools has been shown to improve learning skills. This should be proof positive that implementing a computer crafting program into a school curriculum can result in children who learn computer skills much more quickly than a program that simply teaches them the basics of computer use without allowing the children to utilize their imagination and creativity as part of that learning process. For children to excel in the future, computer crafting should be part of the curriculum in every school that offers lessons in computer skills.

If your child's school does not offer computer skills as part of its curriculum, then teach them yourself! The wealth of websites providing lessons for basic computer skills for children as well as sites that offer computer crafting projects especially for kids makes your job that much easier. Start with something simple like a greeting card or a bookmark. Once your child prints out that project and holds their handiwork in their own hands, they will be clamoring for more. See Appendix A for computer crafting websites geared specifically toward kids of all ages.

Chapter 2, "Tools of the Trade," describes some of the tools of the computer crafting trade—everything from your PC and printer and other peripherals to specialty and general crafting items.

# CHAPTER TWO

# Tools of the Trade

# Tools of the Trade

This chapter outlines all the tools and materials you'll need to get started applying your creativity to computer crafting. It covers everything from the computer itself to the basic crafting tools you'll be using even without a computer, including printers, software, and specialty craft papers. Using the information in this chapter, you can evaluate the toolkit you already have and make appropriate choices for adding or replacing tools to meet your project needs.

The two most important tools for computer crafting are a computer and a printer. Knowing what to look for in a computer or printer can save you hours of frustration.

### Your Personal Computer

Today's computers are far more advanced than machines made only a few years ago. Hard drive size has increased exponentially. RAM (random access memory) has become much less expensive and allows your computer to speed through tasks much more quickly than before. Processors—the "brain" of your computer—have also advanced tremendously. Put all these advances together, and you have the makings of an awesome creative tool!

The process of editing photographs, for example, can use a great deal of memory, and the more RAM you have, the more quickly you will be able to complete the task. And since photographs can be very large files, the larger your hard drive, the more photographs you'll be able to store. But don't panic if you think your hard drive is not large enough or you don't have enough memory. Upgrading today's PCs is much simpler than you might think. And if you have a recordable CD drive in your computer, you can also store files on CDs to save space on your hard drive.

| | Good | Better | Best |
|---|---|---|---|
| **RAM (memory)** | 256 MB | 512 MB | 1GB |
| **Hard drive** | 60 GB, 7200 RPM, 4 MB cache | 80 GB, 7200 RPM, 8 MB cache | 120 GB, 7200 RPM, 8 MB cache |
| **Available USB ports** | 2 | 4 | 7 |
| **CD and DVD drives** | 48X CD-RW | 52X CD/4X DVD-RW | 52X CD-RW/8X DVD-RW |
| **Flash drives (pocket-sized memory drives that plug into your USB port and are totally portable)** | 256 MB flash drive | 512 MB flash drive | 1 GB flash drive |
| **External hard drives (for storage)** | 40 GB, 5400 RPM, 2 MB cache | 80 GB, 7200 RPM, 8 MB cache | 200 GB, 7200 RPM, 8 MB cache |

**Table 2-1:** Important Features for a PC Being Used for Computer Crafting

All this being said, most computers that have been purchased in the last two or three years will probably work just fine without any additional upgrading. Table 2-1 summarizes the key features you should look for in a computer if you plan to use it in crafting.

## Printers

There are only two types of printers you need to consider for craft work: inkjets and laser printers. The specialty craft papers used in most of this book's projects are only available for inkjet printers, so that's what we'll devote most of our attention to, but laser printers are also worth a brief look.

### Laser Printers

Laser printers use a dry printing process that utilizes cartridges of toner powder similar to the cartridges found in most copy machines. In fact, the first copy machine, invented in 1938, was the foundation for today's laser printer.

Up until a few years ago, laser printers only printed in black. That has changed. While they are still more expensive than inkjet printers, color laser printers are becoming increasingly more affordable and can be had for a few hundred dollars.

Laser printers can be a wonderful tool for computer crafting, since the ink is permanent, does not fade, and is waterproof. This can result in computer crafts with a much longer life span than those created with an inkjet printer, which can be particularly important if you are creating computer crafts that you plan to sell. But keep in mind that some of the wonderful papers made specifically for inkjet printers will not work in a laser printer.

### Inkjet and Bubblejet Printers

Inkjet or bubblejet printers are the type most people use for craft projects, simply because they can handle the specialty paper and fabric materials used in crafting.

Inkjets work their magic by placing minuscule droplets of ink onto the paper. These dots are actually smaller than the diameter of a human hair and are positioned on the paper very precisely. By combining dots of different ink colors—cyan, magenta, yellow, and black, commonly known as CMYK—inkjet printers can create photo-quality images.

There are actually two types of inkjet printers. *Thermal* inkjet printers, also known as *bubblejet* printers, use heat to cause the ink to vaporize, and this creates a bubble. Expansion of this bubble forces ink through the nozzles and onto the paper. The typical thermal inkjet printer has 300 to 600 nozzles, and every one of them can fire a droplet of ink at the same time. Canon and Hewlett-Packard are common examples of thermal inkjet printers.

The second type of inkjet printer, *piezoelectric*, was patented by Epson and uses tiny crystals that receive an electrical charge that causes the crystal to vibrate. It is this vibration that forces the tiny amount of ink through the nozzles.

For both types, the heart of the inkjet printer is the print head, which contains tiny nozzles that spray drops of ink onto the paper. Some inkjet manufacturers include the print head right on the ink cartridge, which means you get a fresh print head with every cartridge change. These cartridges tend to be a bit more expensive. Ink cartridges come in various combinations, depending on the printer manufacturer. Some inkjet printers use one cartridge for black and another cartridge that contains the three colored inks—cyan, magenta, and yellow. Other printers use a separate cartridge for each color, and some printers even have separate print heads for each color cartridge.

In any type of inkjet printer, a motor moves the print head and cartridge assembly back and forth across the paper. A stabilizer bar ensures that this movement is precise and controlled. A set of rollers pulls the paper in from the feed tray and advances it when the print head is ready for the next pass.

|  | Good | Better | Best |
|---|---|---|---|
| **Cartridges** | One black cartridge and one for CMY (color) | One black cartridge and one for each of three colors (C, M, and Y) | One black cartridge and five for colors (cyan, light cyan, magenta, light magenta, yellow) |
| **Print margins** | ¼" around top and sides, ⅓" at bottom | ⅛" at top, ¼" on sides, and ⅛" on bottom | Full bleed (0" margins on all sides) |
| **Maximum [?]Media weight** | 60 lb. card stock | 80 lb. card stock | 110 lb. (index) card stock |
| **Media types (special paper settings)** | Plain paper, card stock, and envelopes | Plain paper, card stock, envelopes, transparencies, and other types of inkjet media such as art canvas, shrink film, etc. | Plain paper, card stock, envelopes, transparencies, and other types of inkjet media such as art canvas, shrink film, etc. and banner paper |
| **Special features** | Landscape and portrait orientation | Landscape and portrait orientation, allowance for custom paper sizes, capability to convert to grayscale | Landscape and portrait orientation, allowance for custom paper sizes, capability to convert to grayscale, capability to convert to sepia tones, continuous banner printing, digital card reader for use with a digital camera |
| **Speed (in normal mode)** | 7 ppm black<br>4 ppm color | 17 ppm black<br>5 ppm color | 25 ppm black<br>8 ppm color |

**Table 2-2:** Important Inkjet Printer Features for Computer Crafting

## Inkjet Features and Computer Crafts

Assuming you've decided to use an inkjet printer, there are plenty of models to choose from. Two features that are particularly important for home use and crafting are the type of ink the printer uses and the way it handles paper.

## Inkjet Inks

There are several types of inkjet cartridges, depending on the brand of printer you use, but almost all inkjet printers use one of two types of ink: water-solvent-based and non-water-solvent-based. The current models of home inkjet printers—those with a print width of less than 24 inches—use the water-solvent-based inks. (This includes the wide-format inkjet printers many of us have at home, which usually have a print width of no more than 13 inches.)

Water-solvent-based inks are considered more "family friendly." You may think that means they are non-toxic and non-flammable, but if you check the MSDS (Material Data Safety Sheet) for the ink manufacturers, you'll see that they all have a flash point, which means they are indeed flammable. In addition, most of the ink cartridges manufactured by the larger companies like HP, Canon, and Epson specify on their MSDS that inhalation of the ink vapors can lead to respiratory problems. These problems are not necessarily serious and in most cases can be resolved by getting some fresh air if you've been affected. However, people with asthma or other respiratory problems should use caution. Check the MSDS for HP inks, and you'll see that this risk is clearly stated. The risk is higher in young children than in adults, which is why the MSDS also

### Alps MicroDry Printers

One other type of printer I must mention is the MicroDry. Any of you who own or have owned an Alps printer know what I mean. These printers utilize a resin-transfer system with individual colored thermal ribbon cartridges rather than liquid ink or powder toner, and the cartridges are very inexpensive. Alps printers can print in process color using cyan, magenta, yellow, and black cartridges, as well as using such spot colors like white, silver, and gold. Alps, a Japanese electronics firm, stopped making retail printers about two years ago. Because they were not a well-known name in the U.S. and because their printers are noisier and slower than most inkjet printers, the Alps MicroDry system never achieved wide acceptance, which is a shame, because it produces clear, waterproof, fade-resistant output. The downside to the Alps printer is that it can only print on paper that has a smooth surface, so any textured paper does not produce desirable results.

MicroDry printers are still available on eBay (I just purchased one myself a few weeks ago, and I love the fact that I can now print in gold, silver, and white), and although Alps will provide you with the drivers you need for the newer operating systems like Windows XP and Windows 2000, they will only be supporting these printers through 2006. There are still many websites out there that sell the cartridges, but whether or not those cartridges will still be available once Alps stops supporting the printers is anyone's guess. You can be sure I will be stocking up on those cartridges like a squirrel hoards nuts!

recommends that cartridges be kept away from children. In fact, this warning is posted on the MSDS for the three major manufactures we checked, not just Hewlett-Packard. Epson, Canon, and HP—the three sites we checked—all have links to the MSDS for their ink cartridges. It's better to be safe than sorry, especially if you're thinking of computer crafting for your children, so be sure to take the necessary precautions.

These safety issues aside, for the most part today's inkjet inks are much safer to use in a home or office environment than non-water-solvent-based inks, which can contain Xylene or Toluene—both known carcinogens.

#### Water-Soluble and Non-soluble Inks

There are two types of water-solvent-based inkjet inks: water-soluble dyes and non-soluble pigment suspensions. It is from these two different types of colorants that the terms *dye base* and *pigment base* inks are derived:

**Water-soluble dyes:** These are the most common and also provide for the widest range of color. They are the least expensive to manufacture, but they have a short life span once printed and they also have very low resistance to ultraviolet radiation.

If you have ever printed photographs with water-soluble ink from your inkjet printer and they've been sitting in a frame in a well-lit area of your home or office for some time, you'll notice that they fade quite a bit.

There are companies now making UV-resistant inks for most inkjet printers. The problem is that so far these UV-resistant inks are only available as refill kits and in many cases refilling cartridges can be a messy task.

**Pigment suspensions or pigment-based inks:**
These are most common in black ink cartridges. Most major inkjet manufacturers use this type of ink for the black cartridges in their four-color printers because it has better UV resistance than water-soluble dyes and it also tends to be water resistant. Print a few lines of black text on your inkjet and give it a few minutes to dry. Then sprinkle a few drops of water on it, and chances are it will not run the way your colored inks will.

Pigment-based color inks are thicker than water-soluble ones due to their chemical composition, and therefore, they should not be used in printers that are not made specifically for this type of ink. Eventually, the ink coagulates and causes the nozzles in your printer to clog.

NOTE: *Epson created a hybrid ink, UltraChrome, by combining a pigment suspension with a pure soluble dye. However, this ink can only be used in certain hybrid Epson Stylus printer models.*

### Edible Inks

Okay, so now we have thoroughly confused you on the topic of inks. But there is one more type of ink we must tell you about—and it's *edible!*

Edible inks are basically made from food coloring. Before ordering these cartridges, which so far can only be used in Canon printers, make certain that they are manufactured using FDA-approved ingredients and standards.

### Edible Media

You can print your edible inks on several types of edible media, which for the most part are made of rice paper. The problem with rice paper is its consistency. Imagine printing on a piece of thick tissue paper and placing that paper on top of a cake. When you attempt to cut the cake, the paper folds and buckles and does not give you a nice clean cut simply because it is paper.

However, one company—PhotoFrost (www. computercakes.com)—actually makes letter-sized sheets of pure white frosting! Print on them just as you would a sheet of paper, peel the backing off according to the instructions, and lay the sheet on the top of your cake. The best thing about these sheets is that they actually melt right into the frosting on a cake (which has to be white, by the way), so when cutting the cake you won't run into the problem you have when you use rice paper. Also, unlike rice paper, these sheets have no funny taste or texture, are FDA approved, and are kosher to boot.

NOTE: *Any printer that you use for edible inks should not be used for any other type of printing, or you will contaminate the print heads. Always dedicate a printer solely to printing with edible inks.*

## Paper Paths

Today's inkjet printers use three different types of paper paths. The type of printer you choose will depend on the weight of the paper you will use most often. The heavier the paper, the more likely you should choose a straight paper path, although some of the curved path printers do a wonderful job of handling paper up to 110 lb. index card stock. Make sure you check the specifications on a printer before you decide what to purchase.

### Curved Path

Hewlett-Packard printers typically use a curved paper path with a front-feed tray that requires you to place the sheet in the tray upside down. The paper is pulled in, wraps around the inside of the printer, and the printable side passes below the print head. The path resembles the shape of a letter C.

### Rear-Feeding Path

Canon, Epson, Lexmark, and most other inkjet printers use a rear-feeding paper tray. The paper is inserted upright, from the rear of the printer, rather than flat as in HP printers. The paper still curves when it feeds into the printer, but the curve is slight, at an angle of about 60 degrees. The paper feeds below the print head, but because it does not curve all the way around, the side you see in front of you when you place it in the tray is the side that will be printed. HP printers, on the other hand, print on the bottom of the sheet; when you place a sheet of paper in an HP paper tray, the side that is facing down is the side that will be printed, unless you use the rear manual feed that is available on many HP inkjets.

### Straight Path

The third type of paper path is a true straight path. Most high-end HP printers include a straight paper path at the rear of the printer. This is usually a manual feed, meaning you must feed each sheet in one at a time, but this enables the printer to handle heavier stock than it might otherwise be capable of printing on when utilizing the front-feed tray. Several other printer manufacturers, such as Epson, Lexmark and Canon, are now including a straight paper path at the rear of their printers as well. Canon refers to it as a *dual printing path*.

The type of printer you select will depend on the type of paper you will most often be using. If you plan on doing a lot of printing on heavy card stock, be certain to check the specs on the printer.

### Inkjet Printers and the Print Margin

Many inkjet printers have one important physical limitation that you'll need to work around for many craft projects, including some of those in Part II: They cannot print to the full length and width of the paper; they must leave a "print margin," as shown in Figure 2-1. (The area outside that margin is known as the *unprintable area*.) These margins are independent of any margin or print area that you set in software; in fact, if you set margins in software that ignore the physical limit, you won't get the result you want.

There are newer inkjet printers available that allow you to print a true full-bleed page. Epson makes photo printers that allow you to print without margins on a letter-sized sheet (8 1/2" x 11"). Most Hewlett-Packard and Canon printers still have unprintable margins. If this is a major issue for your projects, make sure you check the specifications on any printer you're considering before you make the purchase.

The print margin is usually at least a half-inch on the bottom and approximately a quarter-inch at the top and sides. Some inkjet manufacturers make it a bit easier to beat those print margins, and some programs allow you to emulate the margins of a laser printer so you can print much closer to the edge of the paper. At the end of this chapter, you'll also find some tips and tricks for

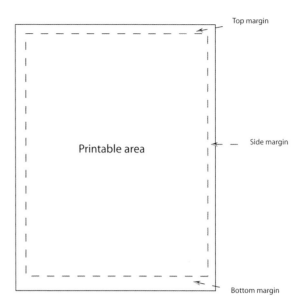

**Figure 2-1:** An image intended to print as a "full bleed" can only print to the physical print margin imposed by the printer.

"cheating" the print margin on greeting cards and envelopes.

But in general, for any project where you want the effect of a *full bleed* (an image printed to the edge of the paper), plan to get out the paper cutter. You'll print your project on larger paper than you need and then trim to the correct size.

The exact print margin varies from printer to printer. Check the manufacturer's documentation that came with your printer to determine the printable margins of your particular brand and model. If that information isn't available, here's a test you can use to determine what your printer's margins are:

1. Open a blank page in your graphics program and place a rectangle on the page.

2. Stretch this rectangle to cover the entire page and fill it with a pattern that will not use too much ink, such as the graph paper texture used in Figure 2-2.

3. Print this sheet out to see the unprintable margins on your page.

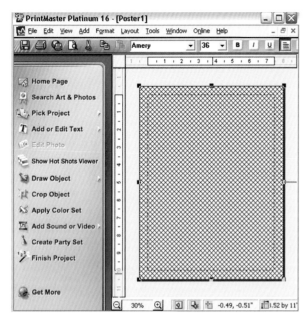

**Figure 2-2:** Fill a page with a textured rectangle and print the page to determine the margins for your printer.

## Scanners and Digital Cameras

Scanners and digital cameras are two other technological tools that you can add to your computer crafting repertoire. They're useful not only for adding family photos to your computer crafts, but also for adding other images that can be further manipulated for use in your projects.

You probably already have a digital camera and know how to load images from its memory card into your computer. Even the least expensive camera today can capture images quite suitable for craft projects. But if you're not already familiar with scanners, this section offers you a few pointers.

### Scanner Features to Look For

Most scanners available today have a one-step feature that allows you to simply scan your image directly into your software. Place the item you want to scan onto the bed of the scanner and use the appropriate tool from within your software to get the image onto your screen. The steps for actually getting the scanned image into your program depend on the program you're using. For example, in PrintMaster, simply select Tools > Digital Image and then select your scanner. The scanner software starts automatically, and once the scan is complete, the image appears on your page.

One nice feature to look for in a scanner is what Canon refers to as a *Z hinge*. This flexible hinge allows you to scan not only flat items, but also three-dimensional pieces, while still allowing the scanner cover to remain flat against the item. Other than that, simply select a scanner with the highest resolution you can get for a good price.

### Scanners, Cameras, and Creativity

The ability to bring any image you like into your computer gives you tremendous freedom to exercise your creativity. For example, I was looking to add some pizzazz to my living room but could not find a fabric I liked. I found a print that I absolutely loved, but it was in a somewhat unusual place—on a tissue box! So I took the box apart, scanned the part of the pattern that I wanted, printed it onto inkjet cotton fabric sheets, and used those sheets to embellish some small pillows for my sofa, as you can see in Figure 2-3.

But I didn't stop there. In my image-editing software I scaled the image down a bit, created a repeating pattern that I could print on several sheets of the cotton fabric, and with no more than iron-on bonding tape, created the no-sew valance you see in Figure 2-4. Voila! Coordinating pillows and valance—all from a computer!

Here's another example, this time using a camera: I needed a graphic of some curling ribbon for a project I was doing for a family anniversary party, but I could not find this clip art anywhere. So I used my digital camera, curled some curling ribbon, and took a picture of it. I cropped out the background and was then able to change the color of the curling ribbon. I went one step further and took a digital picture of a piece of gold Mylar wrapping paper, which I was then able to use to "cut out" shapes such as the heart you see in Figure 2-5.

**Figure 2-3:** Pillows created with inkjet fabric sheets. The original image was scanned from a tissue box.

**Figure 2-4:** Window valance created with inkjet fabric sheets from the same scanned image.

**Figure 2-5:** Curling ribbon and foil heart graphic created with a digital camera and edited in Photoshop

Again, this can also be altered to any color I might need for a particular project.

Once you have selected all the digital hardware that fits your needs and your budget, the next thing you need to do is select the best software for your needs and spend time getting comfortable with it.

## Choosing Your Craft Software

There are two main categories of software commonly used for computer crafts: inexpensive, easy-to-use "creativity" applications geared to home hobbyists and sophisticated, professional imaging software like Photoshop or Illustrator. The projects in Part II of this book can all be done using basic creativity tools.

### Basic Creativity Software

At a minimum, the software you use for craft projects needs to be able to print digital images—whether clip art you've downloaded or photographs you've created or scanned—to different kinds of craft media. Most of the basic tools also allow you to do simple image editing and offer ready-made templates for common craft projects.

The most commonly used programs of this type are Broderbund's PrintMaster and Print Shop Deluxe, and Sierra Online's Print Artist. Although the latter is no longer being produced, it still has such a huge following that it even has its very own fan club known as PALs (Print Artist Lovers).

There is also a wonderful free program called Page Plus SE that includes over 500 free templates. It is available for download at www.freeserifsoftware.com/.

All of these programs are available for Windows only. Of these, I use primarily PrintMaster, shown in Figure 2-6. The first version I used was version 3, back in 1995. The current version is 16, and I have used every version in between. PrintMaster has tons of clip art and photos, as well as a myriad of projects and templates.

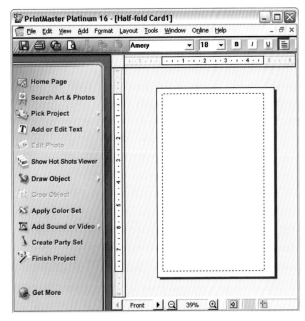

**Figure 2-6:** The workspace in PrintMaster shows the front of a blank half-fold greeting card in portrait orientation.

The thing I've always loved best about PrintMaster is that the Project Gallery shows you what your craft will look like once it is completed. Other titles don't offer this luxury; they just show you the template in the gallery. Being a visual person—as most crafters are—I want to see what the finished project might look like, and the absence of this feature has caused me to shelve at least one of those other software titles. That is certainly not to suggest that other programs won't allow you to create a wide scope of projects. It's just a matter of personal preference.

Typical home projects for which PrintMaster and similar programs provide built-in templates include greeting cards, posters, and banners. These programs may also be used for party decorations, bookmarks, book covers, scrapbooks, and similar computer crafts. The most recent version of PrintMaster has a wealth of craft projects pre-designed for your convenience, including

- Kids' Crafts
- Party Goods
- Kitchen Helpers
- Homework Helpers
- Hand-Crafted Sets

Most of these programs are designed primarily for the non-designer, which means they are easier to use than programs geared toward professionals. They also have the added benefit of being less expensive. In fact, some of the software manufacturers offer free trial versions of the software that you can download from their website. Others, such as PrintMaster, offer different levels of their product, like Gold and Platinum. The pricing depends on which level you choose, but PrintMaster also offers a basic Express version on their website that only runs about $10.

For the majority of computer crafting, one of these suites can do everything you need, including some photo editing and drawing. Some programs even include extras such as web publishing features, email, photo-sharing and filesharing capabilities, and even animated greetings you can personalize and email right from within the program.

## Getting Comfortable with Your Craft Software

Whatever craft software you choose, take the time to learn at least the basics of the program. Because this type of software is easy to learn on your own, and because I can't predict which program you'll have available, the projects in Part 2 don't tell you how to perform a step in any specific program. For that reason, it's important that you spend time becoming familiar with the basic operations first. In various projects you'll do things like draw shapes and fill them with color, group and ungroup objects, and flip, rotate, and scale them. You'll create and insert display text, and you'll place clip art or digital photographs into your designs. You'll pick up some of these skills as you're doing the projects, but practicing them on your own will make the learning curve less frustrating.

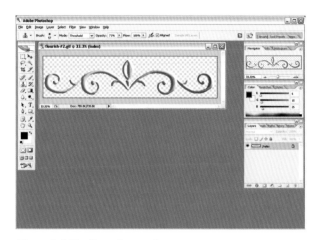

**Figure 2-7:** The Photoshop workspace

Even in your own projects, learning your software before you attempt to do any computer crafting will save you hours of possible aggravation! It's also wise to get used to printing any of your crafting designs out on plain paper to check for any necessary adjustments *before* you print on any specialty paper. This saves on cost!

### Professional Imaging Software

If you are looking for some additional computer crafting firepower, you may decide to invest in programs such as Adobe's Photoshop (shown in Figure 2-7), a professional image-editing program, and Illustrator, a professional drawing pro-gram. These are powerhouse programs that will allow you to create awesome drawings and photo effects that you might not be able to accomplish in the graphics suites mentioned previously. Photoshop was used for the examples in Chapter 1, "The Road to Computer Crafting."

There are two major downsides to these programs: They are *not* cheap, and they have a steep learning curve. Photoshop CS2 costs more than $500, and Illustrator costs about $300. With both programs, many users require formal training, which is also expensive.

Adobe offers Photoshop Elements 3, a scaled-down version of its photo-editing software that provides you

with many of the tools available in the full-blown edition of Photoshop. As alternatives to Illustrator, there are some less expensive drawing programs out there.

If you find yourself in need of these additional, high-end tools, take the time to research the programs and their capabilities before you spend your hard-earned money. If they offer a free trial version, download it and check out the software before you decide to buy.

### Crafting Tools

Many of the basic tools you should have on hand for computer crafting are the same tools you would have for general crafting such as

- Permanent glue sticks
- Removable glue sticks
- Permanent and removable double-stick tapes
- Single-sided removable tape (sticky on one side only)
- Crafting or X-acto knife
- Cutting board or self-healing mat
- Paper trimmer/scorer
- Scissors

Most of these items can be found in your local craft store, but you may have to visit an office supply store for a few of them.

In addition to the basics, you probably want to add some fancier tools to your toolbox such as

- Paper punches
- Decorative scissors
- Specialty craft scissors such as the tiny ones that can get into some of those small areas you might have to cut
- Circle and oval cutters
- Specialty paper trimmers
- Specialty adhesives and sealants

There are a variety of paper punches available, and the more you can add to your toolbox, the more creative you will be able to get! Plain paper punches just punch single shapes; corner punches can add some fancy interest to the corners of greeting cards, invitations, or even business cards. Border punches allow you to carry a fancy cut all along the edge of a sheet of paper. There are some paper trimmers that allow you to get some fancy edges as well. Stationery rotary trimmers that allow you to hold the paper still and cut a straight line have removable cutter disks so you can change the style of the cut from plain to deckle edge to fancier styles easily.

Speaking of paper trimmers, while the "guillotine" type to which you are all accustomed is a definite asset to your toolbox, the slide-and-cut trimmers found in most craft stores for under $20 have the added benefit of allowing you to score your paper neatly and straightly. I particularly like the ones made by Fiskars.

Specialty adhesives include items such as spray adhesives, which make light work of adhering large sheets of paper to one another. Elmer's makes a great spray adhesive.

Another good tool to have is a glue pen. These actually resemble felt markers and come in a variety of tips such as fine, wide, and chiseled. Glue pens are usually filled with acid-free/archival-quality glue that ensures that your paper will not discolor over time.

Sealants are necessary, since the majority of inkjet inks are not waterproof and have no resistance to UV light. There are a few choices in your craft store for sealants. Head to the spray paint section, and you'll find many from which to choose. There are gloss and matte sealants, workable fixatives, and UV protective sprays, just to name a few.

Fabric glues are another good item to have on hand. With any computer crafting project that involves fabrics—a t-shirt to which you apply an iron-on transfer, for example, or sheets of fabric that you run through your printer and turn into items like pillows or fabric-covered boxes or books—fabric glue expands the possibilities for embellishment. A small wooden box covered with a fabric on which you print some family photos, for example, can be further embellished by adding some micro beads adhered with fabric glue. Or iron a transfer design onto a t-shirt and embellish it with glitters made especially for use on fabric.

## Finding Craft Materials: Fun Additions to Your Toolbox

Anyone who has been a die-hard crafter for any amount of time knows that the more you craft, the harder it is to throw anything away! Items that most people would see as trash take on a whole new meaning to a crafter. That empty candy tin can be made into a lovely little gift box. That glass jelly jar can be crafted into a stunning candleholder. The umpteen CDs that come in the mail can be made into myriad of different projects. An empty cigar box becomes a funky handbag. And on and on and on.

Computer crafting is no different. My office is more cluttered with things that I could not throw away than it is with office supplies! Just take a look at what one computer crafter did with the base of an empty spindle of blank CDs, and you'll see what I mean. She added some computer-printed carousel horses, attached a music box movement to the underside of the spindle base, covered it with some pretty satin ribbon, and, as you can see in Figure 2-8, voila—a revolving music box! (You'll learn how to create this yourself in Project 27 in Part 2 of this book.)

So take a second look at some of the items you might be inclined to discard. Start to see them for what they can become instead of what they were originally designed to be. This practice not only gives you materials you can use at no additional cost, but also serves to stretch your imagination. Start thinking of your imagination as a muscle—the more you use it and the harder you work it, the stronger it becomes.

**Figure 2-8:** Vicky Garno of New York designed this revolving music box from the base of a CD spindle case.

### Nirvana: Your Local Craft Store

While the basis of computer crafting is paper, don't narrow your vision so much as to think that general crafting items cannot be part of your toolbox. As seen in the carousel example, other materials, not generally associated with computer crafting, can be a big part of any computer crafting project. The ribbons and lace trims, clay and paint, and the music box movement are all items that can be incorporated into a project.

A trip to your local craft store will inspire you. Just walk up and down the aisles and see how many items can work for your projects. How about some little charms or beads, small silk flowers and leaves, metal leafing and foils, fabric glitters and dimensional paints, feathers, buttons, papier mache boxes, or glass candle holders? Just about any traditional crafting item can become a part of your toolbox.

### The Search for Inspiration

Your local craft store is not the only place to look for inspiration for new computer projects. There is a wealth of paper crafting and general crafting magazines out there that can trigger your imagination. Many of today's general crafting projects can be altered to be made with your PC and your printer. Want to decorate candles? You can do it with your computer. Want to design a lovely little memory book or a child's diary? You can do it with your computer. Want to make some fancy refrigerator magnets as a party gift? You can do it with your computer! Glow-in-the-dark window decorations? You guessed it—you can do it with your computer!

### Specialty Inkjet Papers

Once upon a time, the variety of papers available for use in inkjet printers was very limited. Most laser and copy paper will work in an inkjet printer, from your standard 20 lb. weight to 110 lb. index card stock. The range of papers coated specifically for use in inkjet printers was limited to some glossy photo papers, perforated business card stock, greeting card and invitation stock, and overhead transparencies.

Things have certainly changed! Today, the list of specialty inkjet papers is almost endless:

- Inkjet vellums
- Cotton, denim, and even satin and silk fabric sheets
- Waterslip decals and window clings
- Iron-on transfer sheets
- Magnetic sheets
- Rice paper and foil metallic papers
- Perforated sheets to make your own decks of playing cards
- Paper that glows in the dark
- Holographic paper and mirror finish film
- Shrink film
- Vinyl paper to make bumper stickers
- Velour papers
- Artist canvas that will give your prints a watercolor look

• Specially coated glossy paper that allows you to print designs, add embossing powder, and with the use of a heat tool, turn your designs into embossed works of art. This capability was once reserved for rubber stampers—well, not anymore!

More and more professional designers and printing establishments are using plotters (the industrial version of the inkjet printer). They are always looking for new materials on which to print. Eventually, products created for this market trickle down to the home user. White window cling, for example, only recently became available for use in home inkjet printers.

While there is an increasing treasure trove of available styles of inkjet papers, the sad reality is that the majority of them are not available in craft stores or office supply stores. This leaves the Internet as the main source for acquiring many of these truly special papers. Since you are into computer crafting, the chances are you already have a computer, and with that computer, you have access to the Web. A search for computer crafting websites or suppliers of specialty inkjet papers yields thousands of results. If you're not comfortable shopping on the Web, most of these retailers also offer the capability of ordering through the mail or via telephone.

Check out Appendix B, "Resources: Where to Find It" in the back of this book for a list of retailers. This resource list includes not only specialty papers, but just about every item you will need for your computer craft projects.

I remember the first time I found a supplier of some of these papers on the Web. I placed my order, and the package arrived in a matter of days. I was giddy when I opened the box to see what wonders awaited. Needless to say, I was hooked from that point on and began ordering every kind of specialty paper I could find.

Thankfully, the number of specialty papers now being manufactured for use in an inkjet printer is expanding. In addition to the standard greeting cards, invitations, business cards, and such, things like shrink sheets are no longer limited to rubber stampers. They are also made specifically for inkjet printers. Iron-on transfers can be applied not only to t-shirts but also to mouse pads and coasters, wine bags, pillow cases, Christmas stockings, baby bibs, placemats, tote bags, cloth calendars, team pennants, and even jigsaw puzzles. Photos and other images can be applied to display plates, coffee mugs, ceramic tiles, and just about any other surface, including plastic, glass, and wood with the use of waterslip decals. Inkjet window cling can be used to decorate not only your windows but just about any glass item. Use this material to make small "wraps" you can put around glass candle holders. It has the added benefit of being removable, so you can change the designs with the seasons or for special occasions. Magnetic inkjet sheets are full sheets of magnetic "paper" that can be run through your printer. They are wonderful for making paper dolls for kids.

Going on a long car trip and need something to keep the little ones occupied? Print out some magnetic paper dolls and several outfits for the little girls and perhaps some sports figures with team uniforms, balls, bats, and helmets for the little boys and take along a metal cookie sheet. The kids will have a blast playing with their dolls during the trip. It's better than hearing "Are we there yet?" for the full duration of the trip!

There are also adhesive-backed vinyl papers made especially for printing bumper stickers. Paper that glows in the dark, available with both permanent and removable adhesive, can be used for making decorations, invitations, even glow-in-the-dark iron-on transfers to make your t-shirts or mouse pad light up with an eerie green glow!

Once I began searching for new and interesting papers for my inkjet printer, I decided to venture into the scrapbooking aisle of my local craft store. The racks and racks of colored and textured papers were mesmerizing, and I found myself wishing I could print on every one of them. I had always assumed that only your basic copy and printer paper could be used in an inkjet printer if it was not specially coated. I soon found out I was wrong. I bought a few sheets of various scrapbooking papers, some with textures, one particularly beautiful sheet with a moiré finish, and even some "lace" looking vellums that I automatically assumed would never hold inkjet ink. They all worked! Some worked better than others, of course, since a few of the rougher textured papers didn't hold the ink as well. The moiré patterned paper held the ink just as well as the embossing paper I have been using for years, so now I can add gold detail embossing powder to the text I print, and the results are spectacular.

I've also checked out a few trade shows and scrapbooking conventions, always on the lookout for new and exciting papers that can be used in an inkjet printer. So experiment—just remember to be cautious. If you have a feeling a particular paper will not fit through the feeder in your printer, or you think the texture might be too rough, don't try it unless you're prepared to deal with the possibility of damaging your printer.

## Tips and Tricks

As I mentioned earlier in this chapter, the software you'll use for crafting can be learned on your own fairly easily, and most of the manual crafting techniques used in the projects should likewise be familiar to experienced crafters. But some of the tips and tricks here are a few little hints I have come across in my computer crafting travels that can help you ease the learning curve and let you focus on your projects.

### Keyboard Shortcuts
You don't have to use your mouse for every move you make on your computer. Your keyboard offers some shortcuts that will save you time (as well as wear and tear on your wrists). Here are just a few that can be used in any Windows application:

**CTRL-A:** Select everything on the page at once. This makes light work of grouping items, and it's easier than having to Shift+click on each item individually.

**CTRL-C:** Copy the current selection to the clipboard.

**CTRL-V:** Paste the clipboard contents at the current location.

**CTRL-X:** Cut the current selection to the clipboard. (This is not the same as deleting. When you cut, you can then paste the item somewhere else.)

**CTRL-N:** Open a new document or page.

**CTRL-O:** Open an existing document.

**CTRL-P:** Print the current document to the default printer.

**CTRL-Z:** Undo the most recent change.

### Determining the Printable Side of Specialty Inkjet Papers
Most specialty inkjet papers are coated on only one side. That coating allows the inkjet ink to dry. If some of these papers had no coating, the ink would just pool and smear and never dry. If you've ever made the mistake of trying to use a laser overhead transparency in your inkjet printer, you know what I mean!

Here's a little trick that will help you determine the printable side of many specialty inkjet papers that are coated for printing on only one side. It works 99.9% of the time and will help to keep you from ruining sheets for which you paid good money:

1. Dampen your fingertip very slightly
2. Now touch your dampened fingertip to the inkjet paper you're testing
3. Repeat this process on the other side of the sheet.

The stickier of the two sides is the one coated for printing on an inkjet printer.

### Colored Notepad Adhesive
Special glue made for binding paper into notepads is usually water-based. If the glue you're using is white, you can color it by simply adding a few drops of regular food coloring and mixing it well. This means you can

make notepads with red or green glue for Christmas, orange for Halloween, or any color for any occasion. And if you don't want to color the entire jar, just pour a tiny bit—enough to handle the job you're doing—into a small paper cup or other small container and tint only that portion. This enables you to make several colors from one jar. You can even add a little bit of glitter to the glue and really make some fancy notepads!

### Full-Bleed Printing on Envelopes

Earlier in this chapter I introduced the inkjet's print margin, a limitation you'll become quite familiar with. Envelopes can be particularly tricky, since they are smaller than the usual letter-sized piece of paper. But there is a way around that as well.

Paper manufacturers have come up with print-to-the-edge greeting cards but not envelopes. So if you want to print a background on your envelopes, you're stuck with those unprintable margins. Well, here's a little trick I have found very useful for printing edge to edge (known as a full *bleed*) on print-to-the-edge envelopes and smaller, invitation-sized envelopes. It'll work for any envelope smaller than 8 1/2" wide or 11" high:

1. Instead of designing your envelope on an envelope template in your graphics software, open a blank page in portrait format. Measure the length and width of the envelope you will be printing and place an empty rectangle on your blank page, about a quarter-inch larger on all sides. Design your envelope inside that rectangle.

2. Move the whole design up to the very top edge of the page and center it horizontally. Remove the outline of the rectangle.

3. Now take your envelope and a full sheet of blank paper. Slide the paper under the flap of the envelope and center it along the top. (That's the reason for that last 1/4" stretch—to allow for imperfect centering.)

4. Take a small piece of removable transparent tape and tape the point of the flap to the back of the paper. Load the paper with the attached envelope into your printer per the manufacturer's instructions and print away! Most inkjet printers will allow you to print to the top edge (or very close to it), and tricking the printer into thinking it is printing on a full sheet of paper allows your background design to cover the entire envelope.

Now your cards and envelopes can match perfectly!

### Printing Only the Flap of an Envelope

Similar to the full-bleed printing on the front of the envelope, this little trick allows you to print a design on the flap of your envelope that coordinates with your card or stationery:

1. First, measure the depth of your flap (from top to bottom or to the point on the flap if there is one).

2. Open a blank page in your graphics program in portrait orientation and draw a rectangle that stretches all the way from the left edge to the right edge. Make the height of the rectangle about an inch longer than the measurement you took from the envelope flap and move this rectangle all the way to the top edge of the page. Fill this rectangle with the design or fill of your choice.

3. Slip a piece of regular inkjet paper beneath the flap of the envelope and place a piece of removable tape on the front edges of the envelope to attach it to the paper. Do not tape the flap, because the taped areas will not be printed when you remove the tape.

4. Feed the paper with the attached envelope into your printer so that the printed side will be the flap side. Print your envelope.

When you remove the tape and slip the paper out from beneath the flap, the entire envelope flap will have the printed design.

You can actually use a similar technique to print both the front and the flap all at once. Simply use a removable glue stick to glue the envelope, with the flap open, face up on a sheet of letter-sized paper. The full sheet acts as a carrier. In your graphics program, open a blank sheet and fill the entire sheet with the design you wish to print on the envelope. Carefully load the sheet into your printer, making certain that the envelope is flat against the sheet to which you have it adhered. Once the sheet has printed, carefully peel the envelope away from the paper carrier, and you now have an envelope completely printed on both the front and the flap. You can actually reverse the process to also print on the back of the envelope. This results in your having printed the inside of the flap as well. In order to avoid printing onto the glue on the inside of the envelope flap, simply place a piece of removable tape over the glue strip. Once the envelope is printed, you can peel away that removable tape and the glue strip will be clean.

## The Possibilities Are Endless

As you have seen in the preceding sections, the amount of creativity you can use to create projects utilizing your computer and printer is limited only by your imagination. As you try new and exciting projects, your skills will increase. You will find your own tips, tricks, and shortcuts. You will begin to see other crafting projects and everyday items around the house in a whole new light. You can dress up old items in your home and create full party themes with matching invitations, banners, place cards, party hats, centerpieces, decorations, games, and even balloons.

The following pages contain instructions for numerous computer crafts. Many of these crafts are made using easy-to-find items. Others require some of the specialty inkjet papers I mentioned earlier. Either way, you're bound to find something that will interest you. If you're new to computer crafting, do not be intimidated! Start with one of the simpler projects, and in no time you'll find yourself itching for more. Take the challenge. Let your creativity rule. Above all, have fun!

CHAPTER THREE

# Turning Your Hobby into Cash

# Turning Your Hobby into Cash

*So you're hooked on computer crafting. And some of your friends and family members who have been the recipients of some of your handiwork ooh and ah over what you've created and tell you that you should be selling the stuff. What starts out as a hobby can really turn into a money-making enterprise. Just be prepared for a ton of work! Making money doing something you truly love is the best way to work—ask anyone stuck in a humdrum 9–5 job. But realize that running a successful online sales business can mean putting in a lot of hours, at least during the startup phase. If you are truly serious about making money with your crafts, you have to get into the business mindset. You need to do some research, leg work, and paperwork, and create a business plan.*

If you follow this route, the rewards from all that hard work are well worth the effort. I started my business five years ago, and I haven't had a vacation in all that time. I've groaned and moaned a few times and considered chucking it. And then the inevitable email comes from a customer who is so happy they found my site to help them through a project, and I suddenly remember why I got into this business to begin with. It's like any other business—it's your baby, and you have to nurture it to see it grow.

"Wait a minute," some of you may be saying right now, "I'd just like to sell a few things; can't I do that without running a full-time business?" Indeed you can, and this chapter will help you find the information you need to get started with either a full-time online sales business or a sideline.

## What Are the Options?

Of course, not everyone is prepared to invest 50 or 60 hours a week in creating a business. You may not have a partner who can support you until the business starts to make money, or you may find your current day job quite rewarding. Or you may not have decided exactly what you want to do. Granted, the more you put into the business, the more you'll get out of it, but there are several ways you can sell or showcase your crafts, online and offline:

**Online craft "malls":** These allow you to sell crafts with the least investment of time and money in creating your own business. As in a real-world mall, you are essentially renting space to sell your product. You'll learn more about this option later in this chapter.

**Craft fairs:** These allow you to meet your customers face to face, but they require a considerable investment in the physical setup—the booth, the tables, etc. And just as with an online sales site, you handle all the business tasks. You'll learn about my experience with craft fairs later in this chapter.

**Your own sales website:** This is the route I chose, and much of this chapter is based on my experience.

**A non-sales website:** Exhibiting your crafts on a site that doesn't handle sales is an option if you just want your work to be seen (or if you are selling it through another venue). You'll learn more about this later in the chapter.

## Doing the Research

When I decided to launch The CraftyPC (www.thecraftypc.com), I started by going to the local library and reading books on starting a business. There is a wealth of material in your local library, and what I did not find on the shelves, I was able to locate online. Amazon.com was a true blessing in this area. I also found lots of articles online on the specific topic in which I was interested. Read everything you can get your hands on.

Visit some of the chat rooms and forums listed in Appendix A, "Computer Crafting Websites and Message Boards," and ask for advice. You'll be surprised to see how many people are willing to lend their expertise. I gained a lot of knowledge this way, and I've passed some of that information on to others who have contacted me for help in starting their own business.

Among the books I purchased from Amazon.com's website, four are currently in print:

• *The Neatest Little Guide to Making Money Online* by Jason Kelly (Plume Books, 2000)
• *How to Start a Business Website* by Mike Powers (Quill Press, 1999)
• *The Unofficial Guide to Starting a Business Online* by Jason R. Rich (Wiley, 1999)
• *Starting an Online Business for Dummies* by Greg Holden (For Dummies, 4th edition, 2005. They really *do* make Dummies books for everything!)

Granted, some of these books have not been revised for a while, but there is a wealth of information out

there on starting an online business. The topics you can expect to see covered in these books include

• Defining your business idea
• Registering a domain name
• Choosing a web host and design tools
• Security for a commerce website
• Marketing and advertising
• Legal concerns
• Basic accounting practices

### Researching an Offline Crafts Business

If you're looking to start a craft business that will operate mostly or entirely off the Internet, there is still a lot you need to learn, and there are tons of publications that you can check out for help in all areas. One good place to start is the website of The Carol Duvall Show at www.hgtv.com. Search for show number CDS-1036, where you will find a page that not only includes information on copyright issues as they pertain to crafting (which we will get to shortly), but also has a link for Crafting Business Books. Click on that link to see a list of some of the titles Carol presented on that show. This list includes publications on everything from pricing your work, marketing, legal issues, and everything in between.

There is another episode with a small amount of information on copyright as it pertains to crafts. Search for show number CDS-123 for that information. Or, you can simply enter the word "copyright" into the search box. There are some mentions of copyright issues as they pertain to specific projects on Carol's show.

Amazon and other online book sellers also offer many titles related to selling crafts and running a crafts business. Some of the most promising books I've seen include the following:

• *Handmade for Profit! Hundreds of Secrets to Success in Selling Arts and Crafts (revised edition)* by Barbara Brabec (M. Evans and Company, Inc., 2002)
• *The Crafts Business Answer Book & Resource Guide* by

Barbara Brabec (M. Evans and Company, Inc., 1998)

• *Selling Your Crafts* by Susan Joy Sager (Allworth Press, 2003)

• *Creating a Successful Craft Business* by Rogene A. Robbins and Robert Robbins (Watson-Guptill Publications, 2003)

### Getting Legal Advice

Legal advice and assistance is critical for everything from getting a business license to paying sales tax. I am lucky enough to have a sister who is an attorney. All the paperwork to get my business registered and get a tax ID number was handled by a family member. Of course, not everyone has a lawyer in the family, but resources are available in books and online, so get started with that research.

Some of this information is available from your local municipality or state and can also be found on the Web. Visit the site for your city or town and state and find out what the legal requirements are for starting a small business in your area.

Make a list of everything you need to do, from developing a business plan to pricing your items. You may also wish to check out another book on Amzaon.com called *Your Crafts Business: A Legal Guide* by Richard Stim (Nolo, 2003).

### Researching Craft Fairs

You may decide to start a craft business simply by trying out a few craft fairs. Here, too, research will pay off, but your research will consist mostly of leg work. My advice is to visit these fairs first. Find out what craft fairs are available in your area by checking the local newspapers and spend a few hours visiting them. I learned the hard way not to just pay for the table and lug all my materials to the fair. My website was already up and running, but I was looking for a way to bolster local business. The first fair I attended, I sold absolutely nothing. (But I did get a custom order from the vendor at the table next to me!) I realized that most of the craft fairs in my area cater mostly to country crafts, and this was not the correct venue for the items I wanted to sell. So consider what you are selling and then make sure the craft fairs in your locale cater to that type of craft before you spend your hard-earned dollars on that table.

## Finding a Market for Your Crafts

Marketing your handiwork is critical to making money in this field. If you have been making computer crafts primarily as gifts, you need to expand the number of people you are creating those gifts for. Print the name of your business and a contact somewhere on the item so that other people who see it know where to go if they like what they see. This little trick has led a lot of business my way!

And don't forget word of mouth. If people like what they see, they will tell other people, and it can snowball quite rapidly. If you have friends getting married or having a special party, offer to create something for that celebration—small favors or other items that can be custom created for the special day. Offer to do it for very little money or even for free if they agree to let you print your name and contact information on the items. I did this for friends for their daughter's bat mitzvah, and the next thing I knew, I was getting a call from one of their friends asking if I would do some invitations and other items for their daughter's special day.

Here are some other forms of "guerilla marketing" you can try:

• Post signs with photos at local supermarkets, schools, and places of worship.

• Email all your friends and attach a photo or two of something you can create for them and ask them to forward that email to anyone they think might be interested. I received some of my first orders from this shameless method of self-promotion!

Finally, remember that the quality of your work will be your biggest advertising tool. Don't skimp on effort— even if the job is a freebie! And self-promotion is necessary, so don't be bashful!

### Marketing on the Internet

Message boards where crafters exchange information (you'll find some listed in Appendix A) are another marketing tool. Visit them often and mention what you are doing. But be sure to read the rules and regulations for the boards and rooms you visit first. Some of them frown on "advertising" and may block you from the room if you violate their terms.

There are also "article banks" on the Internet that can help you drum up business. Search them out and submit some articles on the type of work you do. If you decide to develop a website for your business, offer a link back to that site in the articles. If you're going to have a phone line dedicated to your business, place a little advertisement in the local Yellow Pages. The cost is minimal, but you'll be surprised how many calls you get.

Build a portfolio of work you've already done, even if it's only gifts you've given. Have something to show prospective customers. Break out that digital camera and take pictures of your finished projects. These can be sent to prospective clients who email you looking for additional information, or they can be snail-mailed to folks who call. And if you decide to build a sales website, illustrating a portfolio of your best craft work will be essential to getting and holding your customers' attention.

That brings up another suggestion: Start a website just to showcase your work. This is the least expensive way of utilizing the worldwide scope of the Internet. If your business takes off, then you can seriously consider opening a "store" on the Web—and even that is not as expensive as you might think.

The bottom line: Use the creativity you incorporate into your crafts in your marketing strategy as well!

## Deciding What to Sell

You have probably already decided on exactly what it is you want to sell, but always be willing to expand the scope of your services and projects. You might begin by creating custom candy bar wrappers, for example, and soon find people asking if you can create a different item. Be willing to learn new projects and tasks, and master them so you can expand your portfolio. Don't get trapped into thinking you will do only one thing and do it well. It's possible to do many things well and make more money doing it. The more you can offer, the larger your client base will become, and the more repeat business you will experience.

## Deciding Where to Sell

We've already talked about craft fairs. Remember to check them out before investing the time and money necessary. If you have a large enough range of items you can create, how about throwing a home party and inviting a bunch of friends and neighbors? Use your computer to print up a little catalog of everything you offer. Check out local flea markets. Unlike craft fairs, these offer a wider range of items for sale, and the chances are better that your items will find an appropriate niche.

If you decide to try your hand at a website, there are several options you may consider. The simplest would be to put up a site showcasing your items and then add a printable order form with a flat-rate shipping cost that folks can print out, fill in, and mail to you along with payment. Although my website has a shopping cart, and I accept all major credit cards as well as PayPal, some folks are still not comfortable putting their credit card information on the Web. So I give them the option of printing out an order form and sending that in with a check or money order.

## Using an Existing Sales Site

Other options less extensive than a full-fledged online store include online craft malls. Some of these include the following:

- CraftMall (www.craftmall.com)
- artsEfest ( www.artsefest.com)
- FreeCraftFair (www.freecraftfair.com)
- HandmadeCatalog.com (www.handmadecatalog.com)

CraftMall offers monthly pricing based on the number of products you are offering for sale and takes no percentage of those sales. They also offer reporting statistics and several special features. FreeCraftFair charges no startup costs or monthly fees, but takes a rather hefty percentage of your sales. If you decide to go this route, make certain you read all the fine print.

CaféPress.com is another online option. Sort of a cross between a full-fledged online store and a mall, with CaféPress.com (www.cafepress.com), you can start a basic shop for free. They are a print-on-demand shop for customizable items. Every item you sell starts with a base price, which CaféPress.com keeps. You mark that base price up and keep the difference. The nice features of CaféPress.com are as follows:

- They produce the items as they are ordered, so there is no inventory lying around.
- They handle all payment transactions and shipment.
- They manage returns and credits.
- They send you a monthly check for all your sales.

The bad thing about CaféPress.com is that they really only deal in customizable items like mugs and t-shirts, bumper stickers, posters, and the like. You don't actually make any of the items yourself. But if you have designed some artwork and would like to sell items with that design, CaféPress.com may be the place to start.

Figure 3-1: The Store Manager screen in Yahoo Small Business shows you all the available features and reports.

## Selling on Your Own Site

If you decide to go whole hog with a full-fledged "click and order" store—the online equivalent of a local "bricks and mortar" store—there are also several options for hosting the site and handling orders, too many to cover here. I have had my store with Yahoo Small Business since the very beginning. I researched several other options and believed I would get the most bang for my buck with Yahoo!Store. I have never looked back.

Yahoo Small Business provides you with a wealth of reporting features to keep track of how your business is doing. You can check everything from references (sites that people visit to find your site), click trails that show you how many people visited your site on any given day, how many of them clicked on an order button, how many of those actually followed through by submitting an order, and which items in your store are selling the best or the worst. Take a look at Figure 3-1 to see what the Manager screen in a Yahoo!Store looks like, and you'll get an idea of what is available.

While I did have to open my own merchant account so I could accept credit cards on the site, and I did have to open a UPS account (which is free) and a Stamps.com account and make my own arrangements for shipping the orders, I still believe Yahoo Small Business offers the best merchant products at the best prices. In fact, when I first opened my store, I was paying a flat $100 a month and could have no more than 50 order buttons on my store. Under the current pricing structure, I now have an unlimited number of items in inventory, and it actually costs me less every month! They do take a small percentage of some of my sales, but it's minimal and only includes items that sell through the Yahoo Shopping network. It's worth the fee for the extra exposure. They also allow PayPal (www.paypal.com) as a payment option, although so far, you still have to do the invoicing for these sales from within PayPal yourself. Yahoo Small Business provides links to the UPS website, so the shipping for orders being shipped via UPS is automatically calculated. They do not, however, have links to the US Postal Service (USPS) yet, so shipping fees that I offer by Priority and Express Mail have to be entered into a database manually. As long as the post office doesn't raise rates too often, this is not a major hassle. Stamps.com is a downloadable software program for printing shipping labels for the USPS. It requires a monthly fee. But the USPS now offers Click-n-Ship, which allows you to go to the USPS website and print your shipping labels for no fee—just the cost of the postage.

## Designing Your Site

I designed my site using the Yahoo!Store interface. There are many web design tools available, ranging widely in price, features, and ease of use, and there are even more how-to guides to teach you how to use those tools. Amazon and similar sites are also a good place to look for web design books.

Here I'll just note a few things to consider when you are designing a website to sell your crafts:

• Your site should be attractive. Consider what colors and layout scheme you want to use to draw customers in.

• Don't make the mistake of putting too much on a single page. Cluttered websites send potential customers running for the hills.

• Steer clear of using music or midi files on your site, unless you are doing so for a holiday sale or some other special occasion. Aside from the fact that constant music files playing in the background can be annoying, occasionally these files can cause a browser to misbehave and can actually wind up tossing a potential customer off your site!

• Make sure your navigation is easy to use. It can be very helpful to draw out a model of how you would like your site to look, including links to other pages, etc. Make it simple for folks to navigate through your site, and they'll thank you for it.

Although I opted to use Yahoo's own interface to build my website, they now offer an option that allows you to build your site with an HTML editor like Dreamweaver. I stayed with the Yahoo interface because it offers several convenient features. Orders come into your site, and they can be sent to you via email or fax. The shopping cart is included in the package, so you don't have to shop for that portion of your store separately, as is the case with many other online store programs. It's just one less thing to set up. You process the orders, pack them, ship them, submit the credit card sales and your batch with a couple of clicks of your mouse at the end of the day, and two or three days later, the money shows up in your bank account.

It is best to have a separate account set up for your business. Just a basic checking account will do. And get yourself a business credit card if you can, or at least a separate card to use to purchase materials and such. Get in the habit early on of keeping your personal and business finances separate.

A merchant account is needed in order to be able to accept credit cards. You want to accept Visa and MasterCard, but whether or not you decide to accept cards like American Express—which charges slightly higher fees—and Discover is totally up to you. The merchant bank takes a small percentage of every sale—normally about 2.5%—and other miscellaneous fees.

Shop around for the best deals. Don't just accept the first account you check into. The rates can vary quite a bit. While Yahoo Small Business links to a company that offers merchant accounts for Yahoo's small business owners, their rates were not as competitive as the bank I chose.

Shop and compare on everything related to your online selling choice. It's better to take a little more time in the beginning to get a feeling for what is out there than to jump in and risk getting burned.

## Deciding What to Charge

Pricing your items is, believe it or not, the hardest part of this whole adventure. You will usually be your worst critic and set the prices for your handiwork too low. This is okay in the beginning when you're trying to drum up business, but don't fall into the trap of consistently underpricing your work. Start by adding up what it costs you in materials to create a particular item. Don't forget to figure the paper and ink into that equation. Keep track of how much ink you use over a period of time to come up with a ballpark figure for ink consumption. Then add in a cost for your labor and don't be cheap with your time.

Of course, there are limits to what the market will bear with regard to pricing finished work, but a good starting place is to figure that the final price should be about two to three times what it cost you in materials. If the item takes a lot of time and effort, then adjust the price accordingly. If the items do not sell well at this price, you'll have to adjust them down while still allowing for a profit. You may also have to search for better prices for your raw materials. Buying some items in bulk may require a larger initial outlay, but it can reduce the cost of each individual item you create; as a result, your profit margin can be larger, or at least allow you to reduce your prices while still making a profit.

Research what other people are charging for similar items. Check out any competition you may have in your local area. If you have local competition, try to make your prices just a little bit lower, but be careful not to start a price war that can result in your having to lower your prices so much that your profit disappears.

When you begin to get large orders, remember to allow for volume discounts in case the client asks for this. Set these discounts ahead of time and figure them into your overall pricing. You may make a little less profit on larger jobs to begin with, but it can result in repeat business, and having customers come back again and again is very good for business! Keep track of what you charge everyone so you can be consistent in your pricing across the board.

Ask customers for testimonials so you have something to show prospective clients looking for custom-designed items. Self-promotion is great—but kudos from customers are even better!

## The Legalese

As with any business of any type, there are always legal issues to consider. We've already touched on things like a business license and a tax ID, but don't forget about sales tax. If you are selling locally, you may have to pay sales tax to the state in which you live. Check with your state's tax office for information and any forms you may have to submit in order to get on the tax rolls.

Decide how you want to set up your company. I decided to go with an LLC, on the recommendation of my sister, in order to limit any liability I might have if a client or customer decided to take some form of legal action against my company. An LLC is also a lot less complicated than setting up a corporation. And even though you have to file two sets of income tax forms— one for the business and one for your personal income—being set up as an LLC allows you to claim any profit from your business as personal income and makes it a bit less complicated when it comes to filing your tax returns. While I always do my own personal income taxes, I decided to pay a tax preparer to handle the filing of the business forms, at least until the amortization of startup costs was completed. That takes five years, so next year I will attempt to file my K1s on my own (gulp!).

### Copyright and Intellectual Property

Probably the biggest issue to consider when starting a business selling crafts is copyright. It all boils down to what is called intellectual property. The U.S. Department of State's International Information Programs website (http://usinfo.state.gov/products/pubs/intelprp/glossary.htm) describes intellectual property as "Creative ideas and expressions of the human mind that have commercial value and receive the legal protection of a property right. The major legal mechanisms for protecting intellectual property rights are copyrights, patents, and trademarks. Intellectual property rights enable owners to select who may access and use their property and to protect it from unauthorized use."

If you make a craft—say a bowl on which you painted your own design—that design is yours, and therefore there is no issue with regard to copyright infringement. If, however, you create that bowl and you place a design on it that was created by someone else and you sell that bowl, you could be leaving yourself open to a lawsuit if the design you duplicated is owned by someone else. You can use the bowl for your own personal use or give it as a gift with no problem, but as soon as money changes hands, things can get sticky.

A design you create yourself is automatically considered copyrighted as soon as it is created, but in order to get full protection for yourself, you have to register it with the U.S. Copyright Office. Check out their website at www.copyright.gov/.

The thing about copyright law is that you can use any image that was created prior to the enactment of that law. So if you find a clip art of an old Michelangelo painting, you can use it in your crafts and sell those crafts without any fear of legal action. And although copyright law is supposed to protect tangible forms of intellectual property for the life of the artist plus another 70 years, the law is always changing, so if you think you might have the legal right to use an image that was at one time copyrighted, it's better to check than take the risk.

The same holds true, believe it or not, for most of the fonts and clip art you use on your computers. The rights to those fonts and clip art are owned by the folks who created them, unless it specifically notes that they are non-copyrighted. So be careful there as well. There are a multitude of websites out there that provide fonts and clip art as freeware. In many cases this means you can use them for whatever use you wish, but it's always better to check first.

If you wish to use an image or font that is copyrighted, contact the owner of those rights and find out what would be entailed in obtaining a license for use. In some cases, the owner may just want to be asked; in other cases, they may grant you the right for no fee or a small fee but restrict the usage, or they may require that somewhere on the finished item you give credit to them for their artwork.

If you have CDs or books of clip art or a graphics program like PrintMaster that includes lots of clip art, read any legal information on the programs or in the books to look for information about licenses to use the artwork for commercial use.

The easiest way to avoid the possibility of copyright infringement is to use images that you are certain are older than the copyright laws themselves, as in the case of the Michelangelo example I mentioned, or to simply design your own artwork.

Nothing would be worse than creating an item that sells well and makes you money and then having to give it all back in a lawsuit because you didn't consider copyright!

PART 2

## 50 Computer Craft Projects

1. Candy Bar Wrapper
2. Circular Flap Cachet
3. Custom Clock Face
4. Pop-Up Place Cards
5. Halloween Glow Decorations
6. Vellum Fold-over Invitation
7. Notepads
8. Fabric-Covered Memory Book
9. Purse Favor Bag
10. Stemware Shrink Charms
11. Wedding Heart Rice Bag
12. Leprechaun Gift Bag
13. Transparent Mini-Bag
14. St. Patrick's Day Shaker Card
15. Candy Belly Bunny Card
16. Barbie Doll Outfit
17. Glass Sun Catcher
18. Stained Glass Votive Holder
19. Cut-out Candy Box
20. Dreidel Favor Box
21. Halloween Pumpkin Magnetic Dolls
22. Photo Display Plate
23. Notepad Clamp
24. Baby Blocks Favor Box
25. Valentine Photo Mug

26. Rainbow Easter Basket
27. Revolving Musical Carousel
28. Glitter Embellished T-Shirt
29. Baby Bib Birth Announcement
30. Disposable Camera "Skin"
31. Footed Box Greeting Card
32. Scratch-off Tickets
33. Fabric Gift Bag
34. Table Tent
35. Votive Candle Column
36. Pop-up Sleeve Holiday Card
37. Mother's Day Bath Basket
38. White Waterproof Window Clings
39. Coloring Book Greeting Card
40. Magnetic Message Board
41. Photo Candle
42. Gift Card Holder
43. St. Patrick's Day Pop-Up Card
44. Vellum Insert Self-Mailer
45. Wedding Lights
46. Photos in Glass Ornaments
47. Transparent Pyramid Box
48. No-Cut CD Sleeve
49. Decorative Mirror
50. Matchbook Mints

# Computer Craft Projects

Now you get to the really fun stuff! In the following pages, you'll find scores of projects to try out on your own. Some are very basic for those of you who are trying out computer crafting for the first time. Other projects are a bit more advanced for the seasoned computer crafter.

These projects can be done using any of the creativity or graphics software discussed in Chapter 2, "Tools of the Trade." (I've illustrated them using PrintMaster.) Because I don't know which program you're using and because these programs are generally pretty simple to learn on your own, the instructions that follow don't refer to specific tools or menus for carrying out the tasks they describe.

As suggested in Chapter 2, take as much time as you need to become comfortable with the basic operations of your graphics software. In various projects, you'll draw shapes and fill them with color, group and ungroup objects, and flip, rotate, and scale them. You'll create and insert display text, and you'll place clip art or digital photographs into your design. Of course, there may also be manual crafting skills that you'll want to practice as you tackle these projects.

A few of the projects here require printable templates, which can be found in the back of the book, in Appendix C, "Templates." For those projects, you'll need a scanner to import the template images into your computer and get started with the step-by-step instructions. You can also download the templates from The Crafty PC at www.thecraftypc.com/projects.

# 1. Candy Bar Wrapper

## Materials

• Candy bar with foil (I used a standard 1.55 oz. chocolate bar; if you use a different size, you'll have to adjust the measurements to fit your bar.)

• Inkjet paper

• Glue stick

• Scissors or paper trimmer

*Making your own candy wrappers is an especially easy project and doesn't require any special paper. You can make them with regular inkjet paper, or you can get a little fancier and use a foil or holographic paper, fuzzy paper, glow paper, or even just a high-resolution inkjet paper to really bring out those colors. You may also wish to create a few different templates so they can be customized easily. All it takes is your graphics program, some imagination, and a glue stick. So get that sweet tooth in gear and start wrapping!*

## Instructions

**1.** Open a blank page in your graphics program in landscape orientation; this will allow you to fit two wrappers to a sheet and use less paper.

**2.** Draw a rectangle measuring 6" high and 5" wide. Fill it with your choice of color or background. This will be the background color of the whole wrapper.

**3.** Draw another rectangle measuring 2" high and 5" wide with a light gray outline and no fill. This will be the box you use to place the design for the front of your wrapper. Center this rectangle inside the larger rectangle and then move it down so that it is 2" from the bottom of the larger rectangle. Put your photos or clip art and text into this smaller rectangle.

**4.** Place a rectangle measuring 2" high and 5" wide on the top half of your larger rectangle. Fill this rectangle with white and no outline. Place any text you want into this box—special "ingredients" or a message for the recipients, etc. Your design at this point should look like Figure 1-1.

**5.** Print a test page on plain paper. Cut it out and wrap it around your candy bar to check for sizing and placement. Make any necessary adjustments to your file and save.

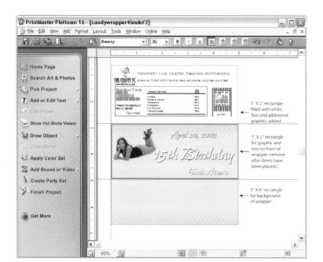

**Figure 1-1:** Designing the candy wrapper in PrintMaster

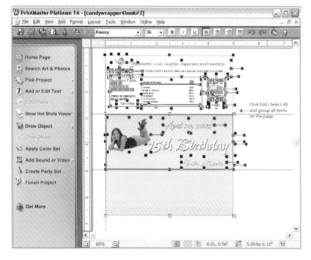

**Figure 1-2:** Grouping the elements you've created tells the graphics program to treat them as a single object.

**6.** Select all the items on the page. This can usually be accomplished by clicking Edit > Select All. Group all the items in your wrapper; the result should look like Figure 1-2. You can often accomplish grouping by right-clicking once everything is selected. Once the items are grouped, copy and paste another wrapper and place it next to the first one so that you have two wrappers on a single landscape page. Watch those print margins!

**7.** Print your wrappers and cut them out with a scissors or a paper trimmer. (Again, if you're making quite a few of these, it's definitely worth investing in a trimmer. It will save you a ton of time and energy!)

**8.** Fold the wrapper over the candy bar and run a glue stick along the edge of the unprinted flap. Attach the flap with the text box over this and you're done!

# 2. Circular Flap Cachet

## Materials

• 4 sheets of 8 1/2" x 11" card stock (You can also use 110 lb. index stock for the backing and a lighter weight for the flaps and interior. I used the index stock for the outside, a high-resolution 38 lb. for the flaps and interior square, and inkjet vellum for the text square.)

• 1 sheet of plain inkjet paper or vellum, also 8 1/2" x 11"

• Scissors or paper trimmer

• Craft knife

• Cutting mat or heavy cardboard

• Glue or glue stick

• Double-stick tape (optional)

*This lovely cachet invitation may be a bit labor intensive, but the results are well worth the extra effort for celebrating a special occasion! Use it for an announcement, an invitation, or a greeting card. I used a spring-colored background, but you can use whatever you like for your background—and it doesn't have to be the same on the inside and outside. That's totally up to you and your imagination!*

## Instructions

**1.** Open a blank page in your graphics program in landscape orientation. Fill the entire page with the background of your choice. Print the background on both sides of three sheets of card stock and on one side of one sheet of card stock. (Two of the double-sided sheets will be for the flaps, so this is where you may want to change the paper type to a lighter weight. Ditto for the sheet that is printed on only one side.)

**2.** Back in your graphics program, remove the background image from your page and draw a 6" high semi-circle, no fill with an outline. (If your program does not have the capability of drawing a semi-circle, simply draw a full 6" circle and then use your crop tool to cut it in half.)

**3.** Place a guideline from top to bottom and center this on the page. (If your software does not allow for centering guidelines, draw a straight line instead and center this. You will be removing it in a minute.) Move your semi-circle so that the straight sits flush against the guideline or centering line.

**4.** Draw a rectangle measuring 3/4" wide and 6" long. Snap this to the guide or place it so that it sits flush against the straight edge of your semi-circle, as shown in Figure 2-1.

**5.** Remove the guideline or center line. Group the rectangle and the circle. Move the grouped image all the way to the right side of the page. (Use CTRL-drag so that the image remains vertically centered. Otherwise, your background image may not line up correctly when you put the whole thing together.)

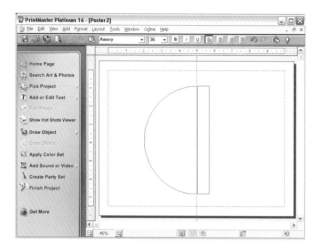

**Figure 2-1:** Snapping the semi-circle and rectangle together

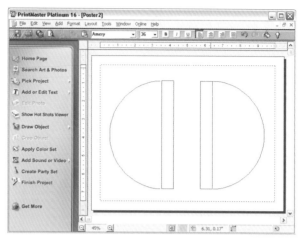

**Figure 2-2:** Final position of the two cachet flaps

**6.** Select the grouped circle/rectangle, copy, and paste. Then flip it horizontally and move this grouped image all the way to the left of your page (using CTRL-drag), again watching for those printable margins.

**7.** Your finished page should look like Figure 2-2. Place two of the double-sided printed sheets into your printer and print two copies of these grouped circles/rectangles. Cut the four flaps out from the two pieces of card stock.

**8.** Open another blank page in landscape orientation and draw a 6" square with no fill and an outline. Center this on the page. Print one on the remaining piece that has the background printed on both sides.

**9.** Now reduce the size of the rectangle by 1/8" and center it again. Print this rectangle on the sheet that has the background printed on only one side.

**10.** Reduce the rectangle one more time by 1/4" and give it an outline of about 8 points in a color that coordinates with your background design. Place

whatever text you wish into this square—for example, the wedding or graduation announcement—and print out on plain or inkjet vellum (see Figure 2-3).

**11.** Cut out the two rectangles and the one rectangle with the text on it.

**12.** To assemble the cachet, fold the tab on each of the four semi-circles and, using either glue or double-stick tape, attach the tabs to the edges of the double-side printed square. Press firmly to adhere.

**13.** Now lay your text square over the remaining square—the one that is printed on only one side. Mark where you need to make the small diagonal cuts to slip the text square into and cut these slits with your craft knife.

**14.** Apply glue to the unprinted side of the remaining card stock square and apply it on top of the first square, covering the four tabs on the semi-circular flaps. Again, press firmly to adhere (see Figure 2-4).

# 2. Circular Flap Cachet (cont.)

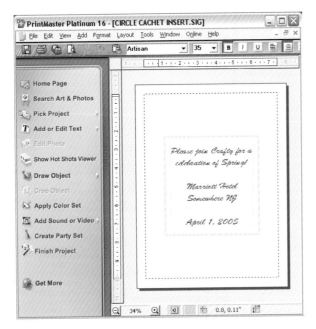

**Figure 2-3:** Cachet insert to be printed on inkjet vellum

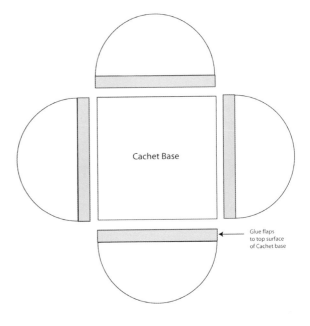

**Figure 2-4:** Diagram of the cachet assembly

**15.** Now, slip each of the four corners of your text square into the slits you made on the last background square.

**16.** Fold the flaps so that they look like Figure 2.4, and you're done! You can either make a 6 1/2" envelope in which to insert the cachet or purchase them in many paper specialty stores.

# 3. Custom Clock Face

## Materials

• Clock

• Card stock

• Clip art or scanned images

*You can do this project with a clock you already have on hand or pick up an inexpensive one to make a personalized gift. The nicest thing about this project is that you can change the design for holidays and seasons or to match your own décor.*

## Instructions

**1.** Remove the batteries from your clock and then carefully remove the face cover. Pull the hands off *gently*. To make sure you can put them back correctly, pay very close attention to the order in which they are stacked on the center rod and the direction they are facing. You may want to write these down. When you pull the hands off, place them down on the table without flipping them; otherwise, when you put them back on, the clock may not work.

**2.** Remove the paper face from the clock. Measure the diameter of the face, as well as the diameter of the center hole that the rod comes through.

**3.** Open a blank page in your graphics program and make a circle (or a square if you have a square clock) with a light gray outline and a fill color of your choice. Center it on the page.

**4.** Make a small circle and size it to match the measurement you took for the center hole on the face you removed from your clock. This circle will also serve to help you place the angled lines for the clock numbers. Center this on the page as well. Save the file.

**5.** Draw a line from the top of the clock to the bottom and set the angle at 90 degrees. Move the line to the left or right, until it runs straight through the small circle in the center of your clock face. This line shows where to place the numbers 12 and 6.

**6.** Draw another line, center it as described in the preceding step, and set the angle to 30 degrees. This is the line for numbers 10 and 4. Proceed as described, setting line angles as follows: 60 degrees for numbers 11 and 5, 180 degrees for 3 and 9, 120 degrees for 1 and 7, and 150 degrees for 2 and 8.

**7.** Make certain that all of these lines cut straight through the small circle in the center, as shown in Figure 3-1.

# 3. Custom Clock Face (cont.)

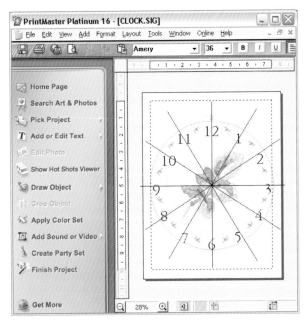

**Figure 3-1:** Clock face, with lines drawn for the placement of numbers

**11.** Print a test page on plain paper, cut it out, and try it out on your clock to make sure it fits and that the numbers are both visible when the frame is replaced and line up correctly when the hands are replaced. You may find, depending on the font you used for the numbers, that you have to move them slightly to get them to line up correctly.

**12.** Once you are satisfied with the placement of the numbers and any art you added, print the face on the card stock, cut it out, punch out the small center circle, and place the face onto the clock over the center rod. Reassemble the hands, pop the face back on, and it's good to go!

**8.** Choose a font that coordinates with your design and place your numbers on these lines. I choose Amery as the font for the clock face in Figure 3-1. Move the numbers slightly toward the center of the face so that there is some distance between them and the edge of the clock face. If you leave them too close to the edge, the frame of the clock may obscure part of the numbers when you reassemble the clock.

**9.** If you noticed a small tab at the top of your clock face when you took your clock apart, make a small rectangle and place it on the edge of your custom clock face in the same position as the original. This is to anchor the face when it is attached to the clock.

**10.** Add your clip art, photos, or scanned images.

# 4. Pop-up Place Cards

## Materials

- 110 lb. card stock (or the heaviest your printer will handle)
- Paper trimmer, paper cutter, or scissors
- Craft knife
- Seasonal clip art

Optional:

- Self-adhesive laminating sheets
- Felt tip marker, medium point

These little place cards will dress up your holiday table with an extra-special personalized touch. Add clip art for a specific holiday, or go one better and scan in a piece of your china or tableware and add that as your design. You can even make them reusable by leaving out the name and covering them with a self-adhesive laminating sheet before you cut them out. Just use a color-coordinated felt tip marker to add the names. After use, simply wipe the name off with a damp tissue, and they're ready for the next dinner party!

## Instructions

**1.** Open a blank page in your graphics software. Draw a rectangle that measures 3.5" wide by 4" high and outline it in light gray. These lines will be your cutting guides.

**2.** Place a horizontal guideline (the kind that doesn't print) on this rectangle so that you have the rectangle marked at the halfway point from top to bottom. This midpoint is where you will place your pop-up clip art.

**3.** Place your clip art on the card slightly indented from the left side and position it so that it is divided in half by the guideline—half above the guideline, half below the guideline, as shown in Figure 4-1.

**4.** Place any additional art in the right bottom corner or along the bottom of the card.

**5.** Place a text box in the center of the card and add a name. Like the clip art you choose, the font for the name should fit the mood of the occasion.

**6.** Now group the entire card and duplicate it three times. You will be able to fit four place cards on one page.

**7.** Change the names on the other three cards and print a test page on plain paper.

# 4. Pop-up Place Cards (cont.)

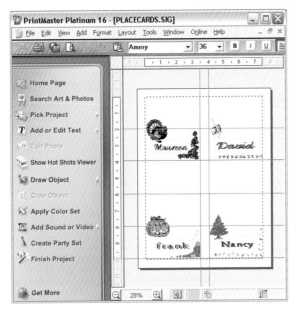

**Figure 4-1:** Placement of art and text on place cards

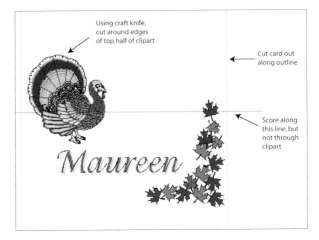

**Figure 4-2:** Diagram for cutting and scoring the place card

**8.** If your test looks good, go ahead and print it out on the card stock.

NOTE *For reusable cards, leave out the text boxes and the names and print the sheet. Cover the front of the card stock with an 8 1/2" x 11" self-adhesive laminating sheet and trim away any excess.*

**9.** Cut each of the cards out from the sheet.

**10.** Once the cards are cut out, score them across the center where they will fold, being very careful not to score through the clip art.

**11.** Lay the card flat and cut around the top half of the clip art with your craft knife, as shown in Figure 4-2. (It helps to have a good, sharp blade on your craft knife.)

**12.** Now fold the card in half and the top half of the clip art will "pop up." If you have done your cards with the laminating sheet, you can now add the names with your felt tip marker. They can be wiped off easily with a damp tissue or a paper towel!

# 5. Halloween Glow Decorations

Ghost clip art from PrintMaster

The camera does not do them justice, but these spooky little fellows are both cut from glow-in-the-dark paper and laminated with peel-and-stick laminating sheets. No bother with expensive laminating machines or clear window decal paper. These ghosts will glow in the dark after light has been applied, and they can be adhered to windows or walls using a glue stick with removable glue similar to that used on those little sticky notes we all use! Removable glue sticks are available under many different brand names and in many office supply stores, making your decorations easily removable for years of use. In addition to lengthening the life of these cute decorations, the use of the laminating sheets prevents the glue stick from smearing the ink on the designs.

This simple project is great for kids (little ones will need help with the laminating and the cutting), and any Halloween design can be used. This is also great for making glow-in-the-dark stars or planets for the kids' rooms. Stick them on the walls and ceiling for a magical effect!

## Materials

• Glow paper

• Peel-and-stick laminating sheets

• Removable glue stick

• Scissors

• Halloween clip art

## Instructions

**1.** Choose the clip art for your decal/decoration and print it out on glow paper. The best designs are those that have little or no color, with a good sharp outline. Any part of the paper that is not printed will glow in the dark after light is applied.

**2.** Cut your designs out, making sure to leave a tiny border around the edges.

**3.** Peel a sheet of laminating paper that has been cut to the approximate size of your design.

**4.** Place the sheet on the table with the sticky side up and gently apply your cut-out graphic, starting at one side and lowering it a little bit at a time to prevent the laminating sheet from creasing or bubbling.

**5.** Peel the second piece of laminating sheet and also lay it sticky side up. Turn over the original sheet that you applied your design to and gently apply it to the second sheet so that the sticky sides adhere to one another.

**6.** Cut the design out of the laminating sheet, again making certain to leave a tiny border so that the lamination does not peel away from your design.

NOTE You can also save some time by cutting your design only once, after it has been applied to the laminating sheets, but it's easier to cut the design from the glow paper before applying it to the laminating sheets.

**7.** Apply a few smears of the removable glue stick to the face of your decal for placement on a window or on the back of the decal for sticking it to a wall.

**8.** Turn out the lights and enjoy the show!

# 6. Vellum Fold-over Invitation

## Materials

• Card stock

• Inkjet vellum or tracing paper

• Hole punch

• Sheer ribbon (wired or unwired—both work well)

• Quarter-fold invitation envelope

This professional-looking card can be used as an invitation or as a greeting and is made with card stock, vellum (or tracing paper), and any type of ribbon you like. It's printed on both sides, so that when the flap is folded over, the design beneath the vellum continues throughout the card.

## Instructions

**1.** Open a blank page in your graphics program.

**2.** Draw a rectangle 6 3/4" x 4 1/4" and orient the rectangle, depending upon whether you want a vertical or horizontal card. (You can fit two of these cards on one sheet of paper.)

**3.** Draw a straight line 1 1/4" to the right of the left edge of the rectangle (for a horizontal card) or from the top (for a vertical card). This is the line you will score for the flap that folds over. Group the rectangles and lines. Save the file.

**4.** Draw a larger rectangle around each of your fold-over invitations and fill this with your choice of color or fill. Or, select a background clip art and resize it, so that it will extend slightly beyond all edges of your invitation.

Copy and paste to do the same for the second invitation on the page. Send these backgrounds to the back layer so that your invitation outline is showing.

**5.** Print one copy out on plain paper to make sure your alignment is correct.

**6.** Remove the outlines for the two invitations from the page and run the sheet through a second time to print the backgrounds again on the back of the paper. If you used a design for your background that requires a specific orientation, this is the time to be certain that it did not print upside down on one side of the paper.

**7.** Check alignment of the design on the back and front of the printed page and readjust as necessary.

**8.** Once all alignments are correct, put the rectangles back on the page and print it out on your card stock. Save the file.

**9.** Remove the outlines again and reprint the background design on the back of the card stock.

**10.** Cut the rectangles out of the card stock and fold on the score line.

**11.** Open another blank page in your graphics program and draw a rectangle 5 1/2" x 4 1/4". This will be the file for the vellum paper. Place a guideline 1 1/4" (to the right for a horizontal card or below for a vertical card) from the edge of this rectangle. This allows you to position your text box so that none of your text is covered by the fold-over. Place your text box in the space to the right or below this guideline and place your text in this box.

**12.** Print one page out on plain paper to check alignment. Once you are satisfied with alignment, print it out on the inkjet vellum.

**13.** Cut out the vellum piece and place it on the invitation, with one edge beneath the fold-over. Secure it with paper clips and punch two holes about a half-inch from each other through the folded flap and the vellum.

**14.** Feed your ribbon through these holes and tie a bow on the front of the invitation. Trim the vellum edges if necessary.

# 7. Notepads

**Materials**

• Inkjet paper

• Paper cutter or scissors

• Notepad clamp or two heavy books

• Notepad adhesive

• Artist's paintbrush (to apply adhesive)

*Personalized notepads make great gifts, but they can be expensive to have made by a professional printer, so why not make your own?*

## Instructions

**1.** Using your graphics software, decide on the design for your notepad. You may want to start out with a simple design in one corner to begin with. Once you've decided on the size of your notepad, divide your page into sections and place the design into each section. Print a test page.

**2.** Print out as many pages as you need. Remember that each sheet will provide you with multiple pages for your notepad, unless you're making your pad a full 8 1/2" x 11".

**3.** Cut each notepad page with a paper cutter or a scissor, being careful to make each section as even as possible.

**4.** Cut out a piece of cardboard backing or a heavy piece of card stock the same size as your notepad. This will be the back of your pad.

**5.** With the pages and cardboard together, tap them on a table top to even out the tops of the pages and place them in the pad clamp or between two heavy books with a little of the top sticking out to apply the glue to.

**6.** With a thin artist's paintbrush, apply the padding adhesive to the top of the notepad. Let it dry for an hour before applying a second coat.

**7.** Once the second coat has dried, remove the pad from between the books or release it from the pad clamp and *voila!* Your very own personalized notepad!

You can enhance them further by attaching adhesive magnetic sheets or strips to the back of the notepad so it can be attached to a refrigerator, a file cabinet, or any metal surface. You can make the notepads smaller or larger, depending on your needs. If you're using a pad clamp, you are limited only by the size of the clamp.

# 8. Fabric-Covered Memory Book

This little book can be used as a diary or a notebook. It's covered with a cotton fabric that is run through your printer. If you prefer to use a different fabric, such as a polysilk or a lightweight satin, you don't have to use inkjet fabric sheets, although they make this project a lot easier to do.

If you wish to use some other yardage, the only preparation for the fabric is some spray starch and a hot iron. If you don't want to run fabric through your inkjet at all, iron-on transfers will do the trick. This project can be customized with photos or clip art and then further embellished with ribbons, buttons, or whatever your imagination can conjure!

## Materials

• Inkjet fabric sheets or lightweight fabric in white or other light color (Keep in mind that using a colored fabric will affect the way your printed colors show. If you're going to use a colored fabric, you might want to use a matching colored paper for the pages.)

• Regular inkjet paper

• 8 1/2" x 11" cardboard

• White 110 lb. card stock (or the heaviest paper your printer will handle)

• Notepad adhesive

• Notepad clamp or some heavy books

• White glue

• Glue stick

• Spray starch and an iron (only if not using cotton inkjet fabric)

## Instructions

**1.** Open a blank page in your graphics software in landscape orientation. Place a 4" x 6" rectangle on the page with no fill and a light gray outline. This will be your memory book page.

**2.** Place your clip art where you want it on the edges of the page. Keep in mind that the design should be on the outside of the pages. Add a text box and fill with lines, shortening or lengthening the lines where you need to so that they do not run into the clip art. Select all items on the page and group them together.

**3.** Duplicate this grouped rectangle and place the second one right next to the first. Again, select all items and group them. Align the grouped rectangles so that they are centered on the page, as shown in Figure 8-1. Save this as "memory book #1".

**4.** Print 20 copies.

**5.** In your graphics software, flip the orientation of your

# 8. Fabric-Covered Memory Book

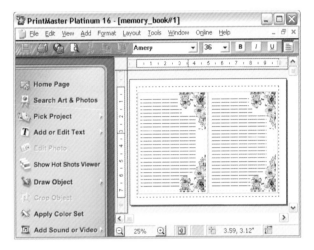

**Figure 8-1:** Layout of pages for the memory book as described in steps 2 and 3

grouped design. Print this design on the other side of one of your printed pages. Check that the two sides are aligned properly by holding the page up to a light. Make any necessary adjustments on your computer screen. Save this as "memory book #2".

**6.** Print out the other side of the remaining pages so that you have 20 double-sided pages.

**7.** With a paper cutter/trimmer or scissors, trim the edges off all the pages and then cut them down the middle so that you have two memory book pages printed on both sides. You should have a total of 40 memory book pages. Stack the pages.

**8.** Cut two pieces of cardboard the same 4" x 6" size and sandwich the stacked pages between them. Place this "sandwich" in a notepad clamp or between two heavy books and apply notepad adhesive to the edge that will be bound to the book cover.

NOTE *Steps 9 and 10 are only necessary if you are not using inkjet fabric sheets.*

**9.** While the book pages are drying, trace an 8 1/2" x 11" piece of paper (using card stock or another heavy piece of paper will make this job easier) onto the cotton fabric with a pencil or a sewing pen with disappearing ink. Spray enough starch on to the fabric to get it damp all over and press with a hot iron. Flip the fabric and repeat the process until the fabric stiffens slightly.

**10.** Cut the fabric out on the guidelines you drew. If the edges are prone to fraying, you can run a bit of FrayCheck (available at sewing and craft stores) around the edges of the fabric using a foam eye-shadow applicator and allow it to dry completely.

**11.** Use the "memory book #1" file as a template for the cover and save as "memory book cover". Ungroup all the items on the page and delete the text boxes with the lines.

**12.** Move the two rectangles away from each other so that you have a 1/4" space between them. This will be the "spine" of your memory book (see Figure 8-2).

**13.** You may decide to leave the clip art on both sides so that it will show on the back of the cover as well as on the front, or you can delete the clip art from what will become the back of the cover and leave it blank. Add a name or photo or whatever other designs you want on the front cover.

**14.** Group all the items again and enlarge the entire design by 1/4" (length and width) so that the cover will be slightly larger than the pages. Save the file again. Print out a test page on regular paper.

**15.** Place the fabric page into your printer tray. Print the cover on the fabric.

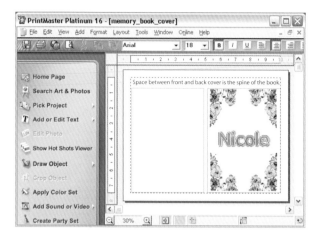

**Figure 8-2:** Layout of the memory book cover

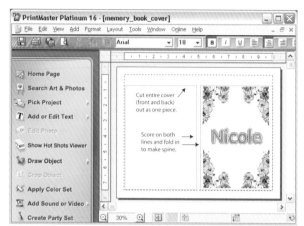

**Figure 8-3:** Cut the cover out as a single piece and score on the spine lines.

**16.** When you cut the cover out of the printed fabric, make sure to leave at least an extra 1/4" to 1/2" around the edges to fold underneath the edges of the card stock cover.

**17.** Go back to your cover template and remove all art from the page, leaving only the light gray outlines of your rectangles. This will serve as the template for the plain white card stock. If you like, you can save this template as another filename. Print it out on the heavy white card stock and cut it out.

**18.** Fold this card stock on the two lines between the front and the back so that you have a 1/4" spine in which to place the pages (see Figure 8-3).

**19.** Take the fabric cover and place it design side down on your ironing board. Place the plain white card stock cover on top of it and fold all the edges of the fabric in around the edges of the card stock. Press the edges with a warm iron to make a good crease.

**20.** Cover the front of the white card stock with a glue stick and adhere the fabric to the front cover. Repeat this process for the back cover. Now glue the edges of the

inside of the card stock and attach the edges of the fabric to the inside edges of the card stock. You now have a fabric-covered binding for your memory book.

**21.** After two or three coats of notepad adhesive have dried thoroughly on your pages, remove them from the clamp. Run a thin bead of white glue down the inside of the cover spine and place the notepad—adhesive side toward the spine—in the cover. Put the whole thing back into the clamp and let it dry for at least an hour.

**22.** After it has dried completely, remove the memory book from the clamp, and using a glue stick, apply glue to the entire face of the front cardboard on the notebook. Adhere the fabric/card stock cover to the cardboard. Repeat this process for the back cardboard.

While there are a lot of steps involved in this project, you are sure to be extremely pleased with the finished project. And so will the recipient of this lovely book!

# 9. Purse Favor Bag

## Materials

- White or colored card stock (I used an 80 lb. stock for these bags.)
- Scissors
- Craft knife
- Cutting mat
- Glue stick
- Ruler
- Pencil
- Embellishments
- Template 1 from Appendix C

*Here's an adorable design for a favor bag or a gift bag—depending on how large you make it! This project is perfect for a wedding with the names of the bride and groom and trimmed in tiny white pearls, or a birthday gift bag with the recipient's name and a small fabric rose embellishment. The inside can be colored or left white, or even decorated with the design that matches the outside of the bag. Just use the templates in Appendix C of this book. Scan them into your computer or create your own design.*

## Instructions

**1.** Scan the templates for the front and back of the bag.

**2.** Open a blank page in your graphics program in either portrait or landscape orientation, depending on how large you wish to make the bag. You will be printing three pages—two of the front/back template and one for the bottom and sides of the bag.

**3.** Center the bag template on your page. Make a rectangle that extends beyond the side of the bag and slightly below the dotted score line at the bottom, as shown in Figure 9-1. Do the same for the handle of the bag. You may also choose to use a clip-art background.

**4.** Layer the favor bag template so it is on top of the coloring/clip art. Add an inverted triangle for the "flap" on the front of the bag and fill with whatever color or design you prefer. Add text or photos to this flap if desired. Make sure the triangle goes from one edge of the bag to the other and that the top of the triangle is placed right at the bottom of the "handle" (see Figure 9-1). Print one copy on card stock.

**5.** Remove the triangle for the back of the bag and print another copy on another piece of cardstock. Cut out both the front and the back pieces *inside* the outline so it doesn't show on your finished piece. Use your craft knife to cut out the space in the handles on the *outside* of the outline.

**6.** If you wish to have the inside of the bag colored as well, draw a rectangle that will cover the entire bag template and center it on the page. Fill with whatever design or color you desire. Print the rectangle on the back sides of the card stock on which you printed the bag front and back.

Figure 9-2: Measurements for the purse favor bag

**Figure 9-1:** Layout for the front of the purse favor bag

Measure from score line to top of arrow

Measure from bottom of flap to score line

Measure length of flap

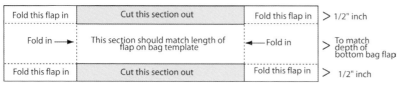

| Fold this flap in | Cut this section out | Fold this flap in | > 1/2" inch |
|---|---|---|---|
| Fold in → | This section should match length of flap on bag template | ← Fold in | > To match depth of bottom bag flap |
| Fold this flap in | Cut this section out | Fold this flap in | > 1/2" inch |

Score on dashed lines
Cut on solid lines

**Figure 9-3:** Layout and measurements for the piece that makes up the bottom and side of the bag

**7.** On another blank page, in landscape orientation draw a rectangle from one end of the page to the other and fill with your desired design or color. This will become the bottom and sides of the bag.

Here's where the measuring comes in. Measure the length of the bottom flap on the bag front or back. Now measure from the dotted score line at an outer edge of the bag front to the point on the bag front or back where it begins to curve back in toward the handle. Double this measurement and add to the measurement you took for the length of the bag bottom flap. For example, if the bottom flap of your bag front measures 4 inches and the height of your bag side will be 2.5 inches, then the total length of the bag bottom template should be 4 + 2.5 + 2.5 or 9 inches (see Figure 9-2).

**8.** Now measure the depth of the flap on the bottom of the bag front. The width of the bottom/side template should match this width plus 1 inch for the flaps that will be glued to the inside of the bag (see Figure 9-3).

**9.** If you want the bottom and sides to be colored on the insides as well as the outside, then print the rectangle on both sides of another piece of card stock.

# 9. Purse Favor Bag (cont.)

**10.** With a pencil, mark all the measurements as shown in the bag bottom diagram in Figure 9-2. Score on the dotted lines and cut on the solid lines. Fold the flaps in.

**11.** On the score lines on the bag front and back, fold the flaps in. With a glue stick or any craft glue, glue the top of one flap and attach the second flap right on top of it. You now have the front and back of the bag together with a base to which you will attach the bottom/side rectangle.

**12.** Glue the middle section of the bottom/side piece and each of the four flaps. Open the bag front and back and lay it out flat with the inside facing up. Glue the bottom/side piece to the bottom of the bag front and back. Press firmly.

**13.** Attach the flaps one side at a time and press firmly. The bag is now assembled!

NOTE *If you wish to add a rose embellishment, punch a small hole near the tip of the triangle on the front of the bag, cut the stem off a ribbon rose, and apply some craft glue. Stick it through the hole and hold in place for a few seconds to allow the glue to set. To apply a strand of craft pearls, use a glue gun and apply the pearls around the triangle before you put the bag together!*

You can also use some beautiful scrapbooking papers. If they are not heavy enough for the bag, print the bag template on the scrapbooking paper and use some spray adhesive to attach the scrapbooking paper to the card stock before you cut out the bag.

# 10. Stemware Shrink Charms

Hosting some holiday celebrations this year? Want to make this year's party easier on your guests? There's nothing as annoying as putting down a drink and then not knowing where you left it or which glass is yours. We've all seen those cute little tags you can put on the stems of your glassware, but why not make your own?

Shrink sheets are the perfect material for this project! By using shrink sheets, and some earring hoops and metallic beads picked up in the jewelry section of the craft store, you can easily make these lovely little stemware charms for the holidays. The charm pictured uses 3/4" earring hoops, but the size you choose will depend upon the size of your stemware.

Add clip art for the specific holiday—turkeys, pilgrims, and pumpkins for Thanksgiving, or ornaments, lights, and trees for Christmas. And you can use the same design multiple times simply by changing the color. Or you can personalize it even further and make the charms with photos of your guests. Now your guests will never lose track of their glass again—wait until you tell them you made these adorable little charms yourself!

## Instructions

**1.** Open a blank page in your graphics program. Draw a 2" circle with no fill and a light gray outline. Copy and paste this circle for as many charms as you want to make.

**2.** Choose the clip art you want to use and resize the images to fit inside the circles. Make sure you move it low enough inside the circle to allow a hole to be punched in the top, as shown in Figure 10-1.

## Materials

- Inkjet shrink sheets
- Earring hoops
- Jump rings (in the jewelry findings aisle at your craft store)
- Assorted beads
- Needle-nose pliers
- Single-hole punch
- Scissors
- Clear nail polish or a clear spray sealant

# 10. Stemware Shrink Charms (cont.)

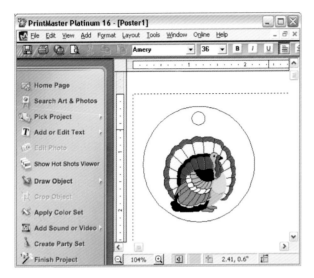

**Figure 10-1:** Leave enough space above your graphic to punch a hole.

**3.** Print a test page on plain paper to check the layout. Once you're satisfied with your layout, print it on the shrink sheet.

**4.** After the ink has been allowed to set for a few minutes, carefully cut out your circles—I find it easiest to use a manicure scissors with the curved blades. Be careful not to touch the printed image, because the ink can still smudge.

**5.** Punch a hole in the top of the circle, making sure it's close enough to the edge so that the jump ring will fit through—no more than 1/8" from the edge.

**6.** Bake your shrink circles according to the manufacturer's instructions. Once you have removed them from the oven and they have been allowed to cool, put a coat of clear nail polish over the printed side (or use a coat or two of spray sealant).

**7.** Now comes the really fun part! Put a jump ring through the hole in the charm and squeeze it closed with the needle-nose pliers. The earring hoops I used have a loop already formed one end, which saved a step. Thread some beads onto the hoop and then add the charm and some more beads. Now take your pliers and bend a small hook on the straight end of the earring hoop. This will allow you to hook the charm wire closed when you place it around the glass stem and makes it just as easy to remove to wash the glass.

# 11. Wedding Heart Rice Bag

See the "Tips and Tricks" section in Chapter 2 for instructions on how to make your own curling ribbon and foil clip art. You'll find a template for this project in Appendix C.

## Instructions

**1.** Open a blank page in your graphics program in landscape orientation. Scan the rice bag template into your computer.

**2.** Place the rice bag template on your blank page and resize it so that it measures 7 3/4" wide and 5" high. Save the file and print it out on plain paper.

**3.** Open a second page in your graphics program in portrait orientation. Place a heart shape with no fill and a light gray outline on the page and resize it so that it measures 4 3/4" x 4 3/4". Place whatever clip art you like on your heart. Don't be afraid to run some of your design off the edge of the heart like I did with some of the curling ribbon art. Add your desired text. (Tip: Balmoral is an excellent font choice for wedding invitations.)

**4.** Group all the items—the heart, any clip art, and text. Once grouped, move the heart to the top left-hand side of the page.

**5.** Select the grouped heart, copy, and paste. Move the pasted copy down to the lower right-hand side of the page. Make sure that none of the cutting lines are overlapped (see Figure 11-1).

**6.** Print the heart page on the card stock.

## Materials

- 110 lb. card stock (or the heaviest your printer will handle)
- Plain inkjet paper
- Curling ribbon
- Sheer ribbon (about 20 inches per bag)
- Glue stick or double-stick tape
- Single-hole punch
- Scissors
- Template 2 from Appendix C

This lovely little bag has a variety of uses. It was originally designed as a bag to hold rice to be handed out to wedding guests outside the church following the ceremony. But it can also be used to hold small favors or candies and placed on the tables at the reception. I recently designed this bag for a 50th anniversary party and included a small fade-out photo of the couple's wedding photo. The art is actually pictures of gold curling ribbon taken with a digital camera. The small gold hearts were cropped from a photo of gold foil.

# 11. Wedding Heart Rice Bag (cont.)

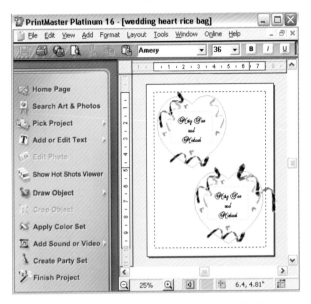

**Figure 11-1:** It's okay to run some of the images over the heart outline, but don't let the cutting lines overlap.

**7.** Cut out the rice bag and fold on all the lines. Glue the tabs on the bottom and side, and press in place to form the bag. Use the eraser on a pencil to get down inside the bag to make sure all the tabs adhere well.

**8.** Cut out the two hearts from the card stock. Place one on the table blank side up. Glue the back of the rice bag or use double-stick tape. Carefully place the bag onto the blank side of the heart so that the bottom corners just about touch the side edges of the heart. Be especially careful if you're using tape, because it will not be as easy to move the bag around if you need to adjust the placement.

**9.** Apply the glue stick or double-stick tape to the front of the bag and carefully place the second heart on it. Be careful that none of the bag corners are showing. It may be easier to try just the glue stick the first time or two until you become comfortable with the placement. Then you can move on to making them with the tape—which is a lot quicker and a lot less messy!

**10.** Gently open the bag while it's still lying flat and place a few fingers inside to press the bag to the heart. Turn it over and repeat to make certain it is adhered well.

**11.** Punch a hole at the top of the heart, about 1/8" from the "dip" in the center.

**12.** Feed the sheer ribbon through the hole. (Wired ribbon is not recommended for this project, because it can tear the card stock when you're pulling it through.)

**13.** Fill the bag with rice or candy or whatever else you are putting in it. Even out the ribbon so that it is the same length on both sides of the heart and tie it into a bow.

**14.** Take a piece of curling ribbon and pre-curl it. Feed one end through the hole and just loop the back half of the ribbon over the front of the heart and twist the ends together gently.

# 12. Leprechaun Gift Bag

Leprechaun clip art from PrintMaster

## Materials

- Inkjet paper (I used a 35 lb. high-resolution paper for the pictured bag.)
- Card stock
- Scissors
- Craft knife
- Cutting mat
- Glue or glue stick
- Template 2 from Appendix C

*This lucky little guy is made from the same template as the Wedding Heart Rice Bag. The only difference is that you will resize the template to stand a little taller. The leprechaun is cut from a separate piece of card stock and glued to the front of the bag in two pieces. Part of his head is on the flap, and the rest of his body is on the front of the bag. This design will work with just about any clip art you chose, so it can be personalized for any holiday or special occasion. How about making the character on the front from a photo of a loved one and filling with some small trinkets or candy? It also makes a great favor bag for a shower or other special occasion. Have fun with it!*

## Instructions

**1.** Open a blank page in your graphics program in landscape orientation. Scan the rice bag template into your computer.

**2.** Place the template on your blank page and resize it so that it fills the page. (The tip of the triangle may extend slightly past the printable margin line on the page, but will still print in most cases.)

**3.** Place your choice of clip art as the background on the bag. You can cover the entire page with the clip art or simply fill in the front, back, and sides of the bag with the design and pick a solid color for the triangular flap … the choice is yours!

**4.** Select the leprechaun or other character that you want to place on the front of the bag and size it so that it extends slightly above the top of the bag. You will be moving this clip art to a separate page, but for now you're just getting the sizing right.

**5.** Note the measurements of the character for the front of the bag and then cut and paste it to another blank page. Make certain the measurements are the same. Adjust them if necessary. (See Figures 12-1 and 12-2.)

**6.** Print the bag on one sheet of paper and the character on the card stock.

**7.** Cut the bag out along the outlines. Cut the slit on the front of the bag with a craft knife. Fold on all the score lines for the sides, bottom flaps, and triangular flap.

# 12. Leprechaun Gift Bag (cont.)

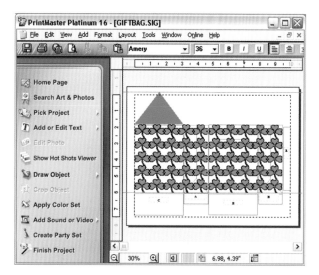

**Figure 12-1:** Using guidelines, you can measure the height of the bag front, which here measures just slightly over 6 inches.

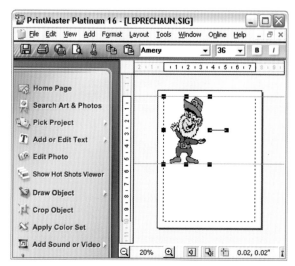

**Figure 12-2:** Using guidelines on the leprechaun shows that it measures approximately 5 1/2"—perfect for the front of this bag.

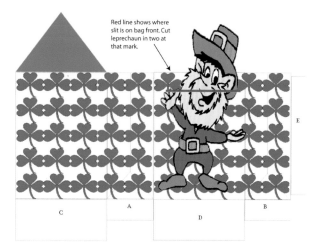

**Figure 12-3:** Cut the leprechaun at the slit on the bag front. Once the bag is assembled, glue his head to the triangular flap and glue his body to the bag front.

**8.** Cut the character out of the card stock.

**9.** Lay the bag flat in front of you with the design side up. Place your character on the front of the bag (the section with the slit) and mark where it will be cut (right at the slit). Cut the character at that mark and glue the bottom half to the front of the bag so that the top of it lines up with the slit on the bag, as shown in Figure 12-3.

**10.** Now assemble the bag by gluing the bottom tabs together. Use a pencil eraser to push down from the inside to make sure the tabs are all adhered. Glue the side tab to the bag as well.

**11.** Close the bag by slipping the triangular tab into the slit on the front. Place the top of the character that you cut on the triangular tab so that it lines up with the bottom half of the character. Glue this part of the character to the flap.

**12.** Close the bag again, and the character will become one.

# 13. Transparent Mini-Bag

## Materials

- Inkjet transparencies
- Rice bag template
- Clip art
- Double-stick transparent tape
- Scissors
- Paper scorer
- Template 2 from Appendix C

*Didn't think it was possible? Yes! You can make a mini gift bag from an inkjet transparency! Use the same template for the favor bag and just cut off the triangle flap on the top. This unusual little bag is perfect for that special Valentine's Day gift or to fill with candy for a party. You can even use them as a place card simply by putting the name of each guest on the front of the bag. Add your artwork, cut, score, and fold and attach the tabs with double-stick transparent tape. That's all there is to it!*

## Instructions

**1.** Open a page in your graphics program in landscape orientation. Scan the template into your computer, place it on your blank page, and resize it to fill the page. Remember not to extend beyond those print margins!

**2.** Design your bag with clip art and text.

NOTE *Since inkjet transparencies have a rough texture on the printable side, you may want to flip or mirror your finished bag image before you print it. This ensures that you can have the rough texture on the inside and the smooth side on the outside, and any clip art and text will not show backward.*

**3.** Print a test page on plain paper and check your layout.

**4.** Once you are satisfied with the layout, place a sheet of inkjet transparency in your printer per the manufacturer's instructions so that it will print on the rough side. Print your bag.

**5.** Cut the bag out along the outlines and snip between the tabs at the bottom of the bag.

**6.** Score all fold lines gently! (You may want to practice scoring the transparencies before you start this project. If you score too hard, you'll cut through the transparency. You need just enough pressure to make a slight score line that can be folded and creased with your fingernail.)

**7.** Once all fold lines are scored, fold the bag and crease it gently. Take your time with the little triangular folds. They actually don't have to have a really tight crease for the bag to stand open.

# 13. Transparent Mini-Bag (cont.)

**8.** Cut a small piece of double-stick tape and place it beneath one of the smaller bottom tabs. Adhere it to a larger bottom tab. Do the same with the second smaller tab.

**9.** Before you tape the last of the bottom tabs, cut a piece of tape long enough for the long side tab. You may have to trim the width of this piece of tape so that it doesn't stick out beyond the edge of the tab. Adhere the side tab to the side of the bag.

**10.** Adhere the last bottom tab with double-stick tape. Gently crease again where needed.

**11.** You can add a handle by using a 1/4" hole punch to make holes in the top of the bag. Add ribbon or raffia handles.

## EMBOSSING

You can add embossed detail to this project simply by printing part of the design on the smooth side of the transparency sheet. To do this, print the template and the parts of your design you do not want embossed on the rough side of the transparency. Allow to dry for a minute or two. Then print the portion of the design you would like to emboss on the smooth side of the sheet. (The smaller the design the better. This will keep the heat gun from causing too much warping on your bag.) Once you print the design on the smooth side, take it from your printer and sprinkle on some embossing powder. Tap off any excess powder and use your heat gun to emboss. Hold the gun as far from the transparency as you can so any warping will be minimal. Then simply cut out and follow the above instructions for putting the bag together.

# 14. St. Patrick's Day Shaker Card

## Materials

- Card stock
- Green foil board
- Shamrock confetti
- One inkjet transparency
- Heavy cardboard or thin foam board
- Scissors
- Craft knife
- Cutting mat or heavy cardboard
- Glue or glue stick

*This cheery greeting card has a window on the front with a "pane" made from an inkjet transparency and a frame cut from green foil board. The inside of the "window" is filled with shamrock confetti! The interior of the card has the same shamrock design, toned down so that the text is clearly readable. Kids get a special kick out of getting these cards, and an even bigger kick out of making them! And this design can be modified for a birthday or other special occasion, depending on the clip art and confetti you use! But make sure there is adult help, since there is a lot of cutting involved in constructing this card.*

## Instructions

**1.** Open a blank half-fold card template in your graphics program. Select a piece of shamrock clip art and duplicate it so that it forms a tiled cover on the front of the card. Resize and duplicate again if you want the design smaller.

**2.** Draw a rectangle measuring 6 1/4" wide by 3 3/4" high and center it on your card front. Format the rectangle so that the fill color is white.

**3.** Draw a second rectangle 5 1/4" wide and 2 3/4" high and center this one as well. Format it with a white fill. This will serve as the frame for the shaker window (see Figure 14-1). Group those two rectangles and save the file.

**4.** Copy the cover design and paste it to the inside of your card. Format it so that the design is faded slightly. This is usually done by selecting the object and changing the color to a shade of gray. It doesn't actually turn the image gray—it just lightens it a bit. Experiment with shades of gray until you get the look you want.

**5.** Place a text box with your desired text on the inside of the card. Color the text a dark green. Save the file again.

**6.** Now go back to the front of the card and copy the grouped rectangles. Pay close attention to the measurements so that when you paste it onto a blank page, the dimensions are the same.

**7.** Paste the grouped rectangles to a blank page in portrait orientation. Print a test page out on plain paper.

# 14. St. Patrick's Day Shaker Card (cont.)

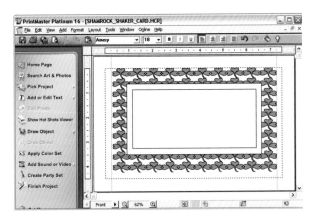

Figure 14-1: The front of the shaker card with the shamrock-tiled pattern. Place two white rectangles on top of the pattern and center both of them.

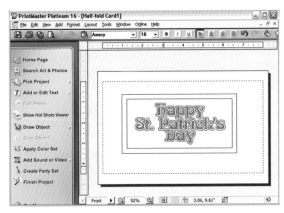

Figure 14-2: Text to be printed on the transparency sheet for the "pane" of the shaker window

**8.** If the frame looks okay against the front of your card, you can now print the frame on the *back* of the foil board. Cut out the frame using a scissors and/or craft knife.

**9.** Now trace the frame on the heavy cardboard or backer board and cut this out with your craft knife. Take your time with this step, because the backer board is quite heavy and will probably take a few passes with the knife to cut all the way through.

**10.** Go back to the blank page with the grouped rectangles and place your cover text in the middle of it and center it in the rectangles, as shown in Figure 14-2.

**11.** Now remove the outline on the smaller rectangle and print this box with the text in the middle on an inkjet transparency. Allow this to dry for about 10 minutes before cutting out the rectangle.

**12.** Once you've cut out the rectangle on the inkjet transparency, center it on the frame you cut out of the backer board and glue it in place.

**13.** Apply glue to the back of the frame cut from the green foil board and apply it to the top of the transparency. Press firmly around all edges to make certain the pieces are adhered well.

**14.** Print your card out on the card stock. Allow to dry for a few minutes.

**15.** Sprinkle the shamrock confetti in the center of the white rectangle on the front of your card. (Less is better than more in these cards; otherwise, the text on your window "pane" becomes lost in the flurry of confetti.)

**16.** Apply glue to the back of your window frame and place it on the center of the card front over the confetti. Press in place to adhere.

Pick the card up and shake!

# 15. Candy Belly Bunny Card

Bunny clip art from PrintMaster

## Materials

- 110 lb. card stock (or the heaviest your printer will handle)

- One piece of thin cardboard, 8 1/2" x 11"

- Glue stick

- Craft knife

- Cutting mat or piece of heavy cardboard

- Clear plastic ornament, 2 1/4" in diameter

- Candy

The kids will love this one! It's a full-sized (10" high) stand-up card with a plastic ball in the belly that is filled with Easter chocolates. The clear plastic ornaments are available at your craft store for pennies apiece. I used the smallest one, which measures 2 1/2" in diameter. Depending on the bunny clip art you choose, you may have to do some editing to create the back of the bunny—painting in all the features like I did in the example shown. Or you can simply leave it the same on the front and back. Then all you have to do is add your text to the back, cut it out, add the easel backs to the rear of the card, and you're all set! Of course, if you're going to be mailing this card, an envelope won't do it—you'll have to send it in a box.

## Instructions

**1.** Open a blank page in your graphics program in portrait orientation and place your bunny clip art on the page. Resize to a full 10" high and center the graphic on the page. Print this out on a piece of card stock.

**2.** If you're using the same clip art—unedited—for the back of the card, you can print out another copy once you add your text boxes and text, but be careful about where you place them. You don't want any text to go where the ball will be because that area will be cut out of the card. The easiest way to make certain this doesn't happen is to draw a circle exactly 2 1/4" in diameter and place it where you want the ball to go. Put your text outside this area.

**3.** Using the glue stick, attach the front template to the piece of thin cardboard. This gives the card the stability to stand without falling over once you "load up" his belly with the candy!

**4.** Press to adhere well. Cut out the bunny front with the cardboard.

# 15. Candy Belly Bunny Card (cont.)

**5.** Cut out the back bunny. Carefully align it to the back of the cardboard cutout and attach using your glue stick. Readjust as necessary. Press to adhere well. Trim off any unmatched edges.

**6.** Take apart the clear plastic ornament and place one half where you want it on the belly of the bunny. Trace around it with a pencil.

**7.** Using your craft knife carefully cut out the circle. Since you are going through two layers of card stock and a layer of cardboard, this may take a few passes with the craft knife. Be patient and be careful.

**8.** Remove the circle you have cut out but do not discard it. You will be using that circle to make the easel backs for the rear of the card.

**9.** Cut the circle you removed from the bunny's belly in half. Then fold each of those two semi-circles in half to make the easel backs. Using your glue stick, put some glue onto one half of the folded semi-circle and attach it to the back of one of the bunny's feet with the straight edge down. Do the same with the remaining semi-circle.

**10.** Now you're ready to put the candy belly in place. Push half of the clear plastic ornament into the hole in the front of the bunny card. Hold it in place while you fill that half with candy. Fill the second half with candy—and yes, this is a bit tricky—reattach it to the front half of the clear plastic ornament. Push gently to make sure the two halves are together securely.

# 16. Barbie Doll Outfit

Barbie's gone cyber-chic! With cotton inkjet fabric sheets and the templates provided, you can make your own skirt and jacket for Barbie with no sewing needed—just scissors, some fabric glue, and some imagination! You could take it even further and make her a headband and a matching purse. Just think about the possibilities! What little girl wouldn't love the idea of creating her very own Barbie fashions with these two simple templates?

## Instructions

**1.** Scan the templates into your computer.

**2.** Open a blank page in your graphics program and place the templates on your page. If you are making the top and skirt with the same pattern, you should be able to fit them both on one page, but you may have to rotate one or the other.

**3.** Resize the top so that it measures 6" wide by 8" high and rotate it 90 degrees if necessary.

**4.** Resize the skirt so that it measures 6" wide by 8" high and rotate it 90 degrees if necessary.

**5.** Place a rectangle with an outline and no fill on the page and resize it so that it covers both the jacket and the skirt (if you're using the same pattern for both). Fill the rectangle with the pattern, color, or clip art of your choice.

**6.** Layer this rectangle beneath the templates so that the outlines for the template show on top of the pattern or color.

## Materials

- Cotton inkjet fabric sheets (or fabric prepared as in Project 8)
- Barbie top and skirt templates
- Scissors
- Fabric glue
- Small piece of adhesive-backed hook and loop tape
- Templates 3 and 4 in Appendix C

# 16. Barbie Doll Outfit (cont.)

**7.** Print a test page on plain paper. If you're satisfied with the output, you can now print it on the inkjet fabric sheet.

**8.** Allow the fabric sheet to dry for about five minutes and then peel off the backing sheet. Cut out the jacket and skirt from the fabric sheet. Pay attention to where the As and Bs are on the jacket and which is the front and the back—you can mark them on the reverse side of the jacket with a pencil. Make the slit at the front of the jacket up to the neck hole and then cut out the neck hole.

**9.** Run a thin bead of fabric glue around one of the A curves on the printed side of the fabric. Fold it in half and carefully line it up with the B curve opposite it. Press gently to make sure the glue adheres. Repeat with the other A and B curve. Once the glue dries a bit, you can turn the jacket right side out.

**10.** Place a small piece of self-stick hook and loop tape (the small Velcro dots work well for this) on each of the inner corners on the back of the skirt. This will serve as the closure for the skirt.

# 17. Glass Sun Catcher

**Materials**

- Inkjet window cling decals
- Beveled or flat glass shape
- Suction cup with hook

Here's a cute little project that can be personalized by using photos or a colorful clip art that will catch the sun's rays and cast a mini-rainbow from your window! Using nothing more than window cling decal sheets and beveled glass that comes in many shapes and can be purchased in most craft stores, you can create a beautiful sun catcher. And the best thing about it is if you get tired of the design, you can peel the cling decal off and place a new design on it.

This project is great for decorating for all sorts of holidays and occasions. While I used a diamond-shaped glass piece, with circular, square, or rectangular shapes, it's a bit easier to crop the photo or clip art to fit on the glass. These glass shapes usually come with a hole already drilled through the top, so all you need is a suction cup hanger with a hook, and it's ready to hang!

**Instructions**

**1.** Open a blank page in your graphics program. Portrait orientation is fine for this project, since the design will be fairly small. Measure the section of the glass that will hold the decal. If the glass shape is beveled, measure the inside of the beveled area.

**2.** Choose your photo or clip art and size it to match the area you measured. Print it on plain paper first and cut out the design to make certain it will fit properly on the glass.

**3.** Once you're satisfied with the shape and size of your design, print on the inkjet window cling decal as per the manufacturer's instructions. We suggest that you set your printer settings to Best quality and select Inkjet transparencies as the media type. This ensures that the colors printed will be sharp and dark enough to show up on the sun catcher.

**4.** Let the window cling decal dry for a few seconds before cutting out your design.

**5.** Make certain the glass is clean and then carefully apply the cling decal to the surface.

# 18. Stained Glass Votive Holder

## Materials

- Inkjet window cling
- Plain inkjet paper
- Straight-sided votive holder or any straight-sided glass to hold a candle
- Tape measure
- Scissors

This beautiful little glass candleholder has been decorated using a stained glass design printed on inkjet window clings and then wrapped around the glass candleholder. Place a votive or tea light candle in it and watch the colors flicker around the room. And don't stop with a stained glass design—how about photos or holiday designs? The best thing about this votive holder "wrap" is that it's removable, so you can change designs as often as you like. And here's a great gift idea … make several "themed" wraps and give them as a set with a votive holder and a supply of scented tea lights!

## Instructions

**1.** Open a blank page in your graphics program.

**2.** Using a measuring tape, measure the height of your glass votive holder.

**3.** Now wrap the measuring tape around the glass to measure the circumference.

**4.** Draw a rectangle on your page that matches the measurements you took. That is, the width of the rectangle should be the same as the circumference you measured. Make the outline of this rectangle a light gray.

**5.** Pick clip art or photos for the wrap and place them inside the rectangle. You may need to resize the items slightly to get them to fit in the rectangle.

**6.** Once you're happy with your design, print it out on a sheet of plain paper. Cut it out and wrap it around the glass votive holder to check the size. Make any necessary adjustments to your file.

**7.** Set your printer to print on an inkjet transparency and print the finished design on the shiny side of the window cling sheet and allow it to dry for a few minutes.

**8.** Once the design is dry, cut it out, peel the backing sheet off, and wrap the cling around your votive holder. Drop in a votive candle or tea light and watch the colors dance!

# 19. Cut-out Candy Box

## Materials

- 110 lb. index card stock (or the heaviest your printer will handle)
- One sheet of inkjet transparency
- Glue or glue stick
- Scissors
- Craft knife or oval/circle cutter
- Cutting mat or heavy cardboard
- Template 5 from Appendix C

*This box is printed on 110 lb. card stock. It has a cut-out on the top with a piece of inkjet transparency glued inside. You can print any design all over the box top and bottom and then print your message on the inkjet transparency. The example shows a box made with message hearts clip art duplicated to cover the page over the box template. This box also includes card stock separators inside the box, so you can fill each section with a chocolate kiss, another candy, or any little trinket you like. It doesn't have to be Valentine's Day to use this adorable little box! And the template is an easy one to work with!*

## Instructions

**1.** You can either scan the template provided for this project or create your own. It's an easy one to make using nothing more than rectangles and triangles

**2.** Open a blank page in your graphics program and set it to landscape orientation. Place the box template on the page and resize it to your desired size. (Remember those print margins!)

NOTE *Be certain to take note of the template dimensions!*

**3.** Print the template and cut it out around the outside outline.

**4.** Starting from the right and left ends of the template, cut one side of the small triangles at the ends of the box sides down to the base line, as shown in Figure 19-1. This cut, when the box is folded, gives you a small triangular tab to glue to create the box shape. Score the rest of the gray lines.

**5.** Fold along the lines to get a good crease. Flatten the box base out again and place it inside down on the table, and then place glue on the triangular tabs. Refold the box and adhere the tabs to the inside of the box sides. Press to get a good seal.

**6.** Open another page in your graphics program, again in landscape orientation, and place the box template on this page. Make it the same size as the box base, but extend it from left to right by 1/10 of an inch. This enables the top to fit over the box base easily.

# 19. Cut-Out Candy Box (cont.)

Snip along all red lines

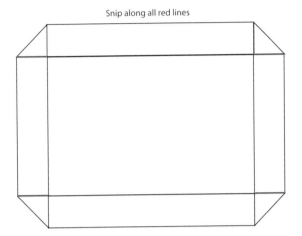

**Figure 19-1:** Cutting one side of the triangles makes flaps to put the box sides together.

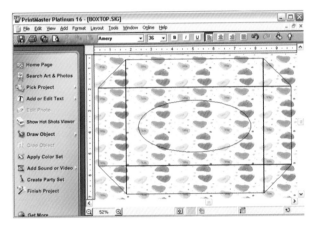

**Figure 19-2:** Resize the top of the box a tiny bit larger than the bottom so it fits well. If your background design obscures the cutting lines, layer the background behind the lines.

**7.** Place an oval in the center of the template. This is the area you will cut out of the box top and to which you will glue the inkjet transparency.

**8.** Pick the clip art you want to use on your box and then duplicate it so that it covers the entire page. If your background design blocks out the cutting lines, layer the background behind the lines (see Figure 19-2). Print out a test sheet on plain paper.

**9.** Once you are satisfied with the layout of your box top, print it out on the card stock and cut out along the outside lines. Again, snip the small triangles and the ends, but this time, cut from the top and bottom instead of from the right and left sides. This will keep the glued tabs from "catching" on one another when you put the top on the box.

**10.** Place the cut-out box top on your cutting mat or heavy cardboard and using a craft knife or an oval/circle cutter, cut out the oval shape on the top of the box.

**11.** Score all the gray lines and fold to get a good crease, but do not assemble the box top yet.

**12.** Using the box top template, remove the clip art from the design and put in the text that you want to show on the inkjet transparency. Resize and shape the text so that it fits inside the oval on the box top template, as shown in Figure 19-3. Print this on an inkjet transparency sheet, making sure that you are printing on the rougher side and have made the necessary adjustments to your printer. Print at Best quality mode and set the paper for Inkjet transparencies.

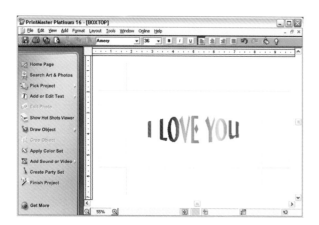
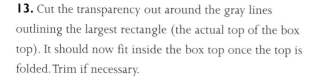

**Figure 19-3:** Use the box top template to size the text for your transparency "window."

**Figure 19-4:** Print on an inkjet transparency sheet and cut out along the red lines. Glue this to the inside of your box top.

**13.** Cut the transparency out around the gray lines outlining the largest rectangle (the actual top of the box top). It should now fit inside the box top once the top is folded. Trim if necessary.

**14.** Flatten the box top that you printed in step 8 and place it design side down. Using your glue or glue stick, place some adhesive on the inside part of the box top where you will glue the transparency. Make sure you get the glue close to the edges of the oval cut-out.

**15.** Place the transparency on the inside of the box top so that your text shows through the cut-out on the other side (see Figure 19-4). Check the position and press it in place.

**16.** Now you can assemble the box top. Glue the small triangular tabs as in step 5.

**17.** You can add small separators to the inside of the box by cutting strips of card stock the same length and height as the box and snipping them about 2/3 of the way up at equal intervals along the strip. Then do the same with strips the same length and height as the smaller sides of the box. Slide them together at the snipped cut and place the separator inside the box. You will have small compartments into which you can place individual pieces of candy. If you want your separators sturdier, double up the paper and glue them together before snipping.

# 20. Dreidel Favor Box

## Materials

- 110 lb. card stock (or the heaviest your printer will handle)

- Drinking straw

- Glue, glue stick, or glue pen

- Scissors

- Craft knife

- Template 6 from Appendix C

This little favor box is made from nothing more than card stock and a drinking straw! The blank template is provided in Appendix C. You just add your own art, print it, cut it out, fold and glue the tabs together, and insert the straw in the top! Then fill with candy or small toys, and this makes the perfect favor for Hanukkah!

## Instructions

**1.** Scan the template into your computer and save the file.

**2.** Open a blank page in your graphics program in landscape orientation. Import the template and resize it to exactly 10.4" wide by 7.22" high (or 999 x 693 pixels). Using exactly these dimensions ensures that the small circle for the drinking straw will be the right size. Make sure that you have the template placed on the page to allow for any unprintable margins, as shown in Figure 20-1.

**3.** Add the desired lettering or clip art to the sides of the box template. (We used clip art of Hebrew letters.) Save the file.

**4.** Print a test page on plain paper.

**5.** Once you are satisfied with the placement, print the box on the card stock.

**6.** Cut out along all the outer lines and, using a craft knife, cut out the small circle on the box top. Save the scrap. You'll need a small square to anchor the drinking straw.

**7.** Fold along all tab lines. Fold all sides, top, and bottom, as well as the flap on the box top.

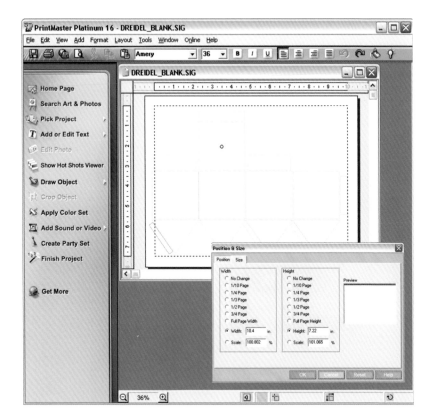

**Figure 20-1:** PrintMaster provides a separate window for resizing. You can enter exact measurements or percentages to resize images.

**8.** Lay the box out flat, printed side up, and apply glue to the four tabs on the triangles (box bottom) and the tab on the side of the box. Carefully begin to adhere the bottom triangles to one another and then adhere the side tab.

**9.** Cut four small slits around the bottom of the drinking straw from bottom to top. Spread the four resulting tabs and fold them back so that they will keep the straw from sliding out of the box top. Insert the straw through the hole from the inside out and pull until the tabs are resting on the inside of the box top.

**10.** Cut a small square of card stock (approximately 1 to 1 1/2" square) from the scrap pieces and cover one side with glue. Press this in place on the inside of the box top, covering the tabs on the bottom of the straw, and hold it in place for a few minutes to allow the glue to set before closing the box top. Trim a few inches off the top of the straw.

# 21. Halloween Pumpkin Magnetic Dolls

## Materials

• Magnetic inkjet sheets

• Halloween clip art

• Scissors

• Inkjet overcoat spray or other spray sealant (This is optional; it will prevent the ink from smearing with use.)

*Here's "Mr. Pumpkin Head"—a Halloween Pumpkin Magnetic Paper Doll with various body parts that will keep your little ones happily occupied for hours! Use a metal cookie sheet or any metal surface and let the kids dream up all sorts of kooky variations. You can use your graphics program's clip-art collection to add your own variations. Why not let the little ones help in choosing what parts they want? Add hats, other clothing—whatever their imaginations can dream up!*

## Instructions

**1.** Open a blank page in your graphics program in landscape orientation. If you're using your own clip art, place the different items—the basic pumpkin, the arms and legs, eyes, and so on—on the page with enough room between them to allow for easy cutting.

**2.** Print a test page on plain paper to check for sizing and spacing.

**3.** Once you're satisfied with the placement and spacing, save the file and print it on a magnetic inkjet sheet. Allow to dry for about five minutes. If you wish to make these pieces water-resistant, spray with a light coat or two of inkjet overcoat spray or sealant. Don't spray too heavily, or it will stiffen the magnetic pieces.

**4.** Cut the pieces out and let your kids have a ball with their "Mr. Pumpkin Head" on the front of the fridge, a metal cookie tray, or any other metal surface!

# 22. Photo Display Plate

**Materials**

• Waterslip decals

• Decal finishing spray

• Blank dinner/luncheon plate

*Waterslip decals can be used to make beautiful display plates with photographs, clip art, or just about anything you can scan into your PC. This is a great project to do with a scanned wedding invitation, photos of the grandkids for a birthday present, or pictures of your pets! You can also match your home décor by scanning or taking digital photos of your wallpaper, curtains, upholstery, etc.*

## Instructions

**1.** Open a blank page in your graphics program in portrait orientation. Design the image using your graphics software. Draw a circle that measures about 5 1/4". Place the circle over your design. You'll be cutting the circle out once the decal is completed.

**2.** Test print the design a few times on regular paper, cut it out until you are satisfied with the size, and fit it on the center of the plate.

**3.** Once you are satisfied with your layout and size, print your design on a decal sheet.

**4.** Allow the decal to dry for about 10 minutes and coat with decal finishing spray as per the manufacturer's instructions. Make certain this is done in a well-ventilated area! (Kids, let your parents handle this part.) Three light coats with an hour drying time after each should do it.

**5.** When your decal is thoroughly dry, cut it out. Leave a small border around the edge of the decal (about 1/8"). This will prevent the possibility of any ink running when you soak the decal before placing it on the plate.

**6.** Following the manufacturer's instructions, soak the decal and gently shake it out. Place the decal on the center of the plate and *very slowly and gently* begin to slide the backing out from under the decal, keeping the decal on the center of the plate. Remember: Move the *backing*, not the decal. This helps prevent the edges of the decal from rolling under.

**7.** Once the decal is in place, blot it *very gently* with a wad of soft facial tissue. Don't worry if you see any small wrinkles or bubbles. You can gently work some of them out by moving the decal, but they usually disappear when the decal is thoroughly dry and adhered to the plate. Let the plate dry flat and cure for 24 hours.

Admire your handiwork! Now all you need is a display stand, a plate hanger, or a plate rack, and a good spot for all to admire your creativity!

You can also experiment with adding text or designs to the edges of the plates by formatting the text or design into a curve that can be applied above and below the photo. Always remember to print out a few test runs on plain paper before you print on the decal sheets.

# 23. Notepad Clamp

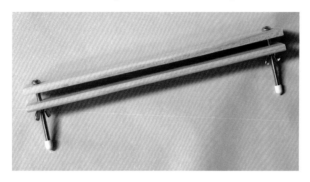

This project is not made using your computer, but in four simple steps you'll have a tool for making notepads much more easily. Constructing this clamp is simple if you have a hand saw and a power drill (or a friend who has them!).

## Instructions

**1.** Cut the wood into two 12-inch pieces.

**2.** Sand all the edges of the two pieces of wood until they are smooth.

**3.** Mark a point 1 inch in from each end of one piece of wood. Place the two pieces together and drill a hole wide enough to accommodate the 1/4" bolt through both pieces at the marked points.

**4.** Place the bolts through the holes so that the two pieces of wood are sandwiched together. Attach the wing nuts to the bottom of the bolts.

You now have a pad clamp! Simply loosen the wing nuts, pull the two pieces of wood apart, insert your notepad, and tighten the wing nuts so that the two pieces of wood are tight against the pad. Remember to leave a little of the top edge of the pad sticking out so you can apply the padding adhesive easily.

## Materials

• A piece of wood 2 feet long, 3/8" thick x 1 1/2" wide (I use pine, but you can use a harder wood to prevent bending if you make very thick notepads.)

• 2 stainless steel or galvanized bolts 1/4" x 2" long (longer if you will be making very thick notepads)

• 2 stainless steel or galvanized 1/4" wing nuts

• 2 plastic caps for bolts

• Hand saw

• Power drill

# 24. Baby Blocks Favor Box

## Materials

• 110 lb. card stock (or the heaviest your printer will handle)

• Glue, glue stick, or glue pen

• Scissors

• Clip art

• Template 7 from Appendix C

*These little "blocks" are actually card stock boxes made to hold favors. The nice thing about them is they can be designed to spell out a special message. Why not include the name of the mom-to-be? Or use them for baby's first birthday and spell out your little one's name.*

## Instructions

**1.** Scan the template into your computer and save the file.

**2.** Open a blank page in your graphics program in landscape orientation and import the template onto this page. If you need to resize the image, make it exactly 9.55" x 7.96" and center it on the page. Depending on your particular printer, you may be a bit outside the printable margins on the height of the template, but it will not affect the project.

**3.** Place your letters or clip art in the squares that make up the sides, top, and bottom of the box, as shown in Figure 24-1.

NOTE *If you're spelling out a message with these boxes, it's a good idea to write it out first to decide how many of each letter you will need and the colors of those letters. Otherwise you may wind up with several letters in a row being the same color. As you can see in the finished project, I found this out the hard way!*

**4.** Print out a test page on plain paper. If you're satisfied with the placement, go ahead and print it out on card stock.

**5.** Cut the box along all the gray lines. Fold all edges to shape the box.

**6.** Apply glue to the end tab (at the end of the row of four squares) and adhere the tab to the side. Press in place.

**7.** If you decide you also want to glue the bottom of the box, apply glue to the appropriate tabs and stick them together. This is where a pencil with an eraser comes in handy. You can use the eraser to press the tabs in place from the inside of the box.

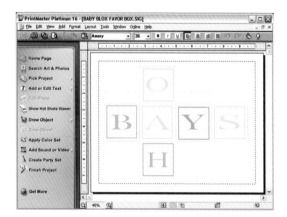

**Figure 24-1:** The baby blocks template, with letters and colored outlines

# 25. Valentine Photo Mug

*Want to hear "oohs" and "aahs" when you give your valentine a handmade gift? This photo Valentine's Day mug filled with chocolate kisses is sure to be a big hit! No one will believe you made it yourself! The mug is decorated with a photo inside a heart outline, and smaller hearts are scattered over the rest of the mug. With any white coffee mug and waterslip decals, this is an easy project. The problem will be keeping up with the demand once everyone sees it!*

## Instructions

**1.** Open a blank page in your graphics program in portrait orientation. Place your scanned photo on the page near the top so you don't waste any of the decal paper. Place a heart outline around the photo and color the outline red. If you're using PrintMaster, select a heart shape from the Draw Object menu (see Figure 25-1). Resize the photo and outline so that they will fit on the mug. (Measure your mug from top to bottom to get a good fit.)

**2.** Place a smaller heart with a red fill on the same page. Duplicate this heart so that you have about 10 of them.

**3.** Print the page out on plain paper to make sure it looks the way you want. Then print it on the waterslip decal. Use white decals if you're putting the designs on a colored mug.

**4.** Allow the decal sheet to dry for about 15 minutes before applying the first coat of finishing spray. Let each coat dry for at least an hour before applying the next coat. Apply a total of at least three coats. You want a sturdy decal that will withstand numerous hand washings. (Remember: Waterslip decals are not recommended for the dishwasher!)

## Materials

- Mug
- Waterslip decals
- Decal finishing/inkjet overcoat spray
- Photo (scanned or on disk)
- Heart clip art

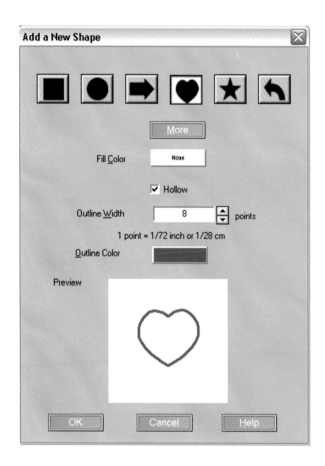

**Figure 25-1:** The Draw Object menu in PrintMaster allows you to change the color of the fill and outline, or delete either of the two. You can also change the fill to any of a large selection of textures included with the program, or even use your own photographs as fill.

**5.** Once the decals are thoroughly dry, cut out the photo heart and the 10 smaller hearts. Decide where you want to place the photo heart first.

**6.** Soak the decal in room temperature water for about 15 to 20 seconds. Shake it out gently, and holding it over the mug, slowly slide the decal until part of it is sticking out from the backing. Place this part of the decal on the mug, and then slowly and gently slide the backing out from under the decal. The decal moves freely while it's still wet, so don't worry if the positioning isn't perfect at first. You can reposition it; just remember to go slowly and gently!

**7.** Once you have the decal positioned where you want it, blot—again gently—with a soft tissue. Any small bubbles will disappear when the decal dries fully on the mug.

**8.** Repeat step 6 for all the smaller hearts.

**9.** Let the mug dry thoroughly for 24 hours. Fill with chocolate kisses or other goodies. Wrap the whole thing in some pink or red cellophane and top with a red bow, and you've got a gift that all will envy!

# 26. Rainbow Easter Basket

## Materials

- 110 lb. card stock (or the heaviest your printer will handle)
- Paper trimmer or scissors
- Glue stick
- Plain paper or Easter grass from your local craft store

*This little Easter basket is made from card stock! It measures about 4 1/2" long, 3 3/4" deep, and 4" high. The strips are printed in a rainbow fill for the body of the basket and solid fill strips for the top edge and the handle. It's even filled with "grass" made from a sheet of regular paper, printed green on both sides, and cut into slivers with a paper trimmer.*

## Instructions

**1.** Open a blank page in your graphics program. Draw a rectangle 3/4" wide and 8" long. Fill it with a pastel rainbow fill and no outline.

**2.** Copy and paste this rectangle three times so that you have a total of four filled strips lined up right next to one another. These will become the front and back of the basket. Group the four rectangles and center them on the page, as shown in Figure 26-1. Print this on a sheet of card stock.

**3.** Print the same page on the other side of the card stock. Be sure you feed the paper in so that it prints the same as the first side and the colored bars will align. This will depend on your printer manufacturer.

**4.** Open another blank page and draw a rectangle 3/4" wide and 9" long. Again, fill with a pastel rainbow fill and no outline. Copy and paste twice so that you have a total of three of these longer strips side by side. These will be the sides of the basket. Group them and center them on the page. Print this page on another piece of card stock, again on both sides.

**5.** Now you need to make a 17" strip that will weave around all four sides of the basket. This will entail gluing two strips together to get the length you need. Open another blank page and draw a rectangle 3/4" wide by 9" long with a rainbow fill and no outline. Copy and paste this rectangle once so that you have a total of two. Group and center on the page. Print again on both sides of one sheet of card stock.

**6.** You need to make another 17" strip for the top edging. You can use the page with the rectangles you made in the last step, just change the fill to a pastel solid with no outline and increase the width to 1 1/2", since you'll be folding this strip in half lengthwise so that it folds over the tops of the rainbow strips. Print this out on one side of a sheet of card stock.

**7.** Open another blank page and draw a rectangle 1 1/2" wide by 9" long, solid pastel fill and no outline. This will be the handle. (Once you've cut it out, you're going to fold it in half lengthwise so that it has some added strength.) Print this on one side of a sheet of card stock.

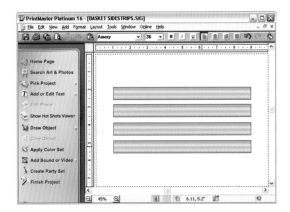

**Figure 26-1:** The four strips that will become the front and back of the basket.

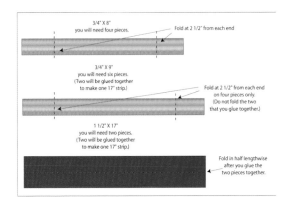

**Figure 26-2:** This diagram shows you how many pieces of each strip to print and cut, and where to fold them.

**8.** Cut out all the strips. Take the four shorter rainbow strips and fold them at 2 1/2" from each end.

**9.** Take the three longer rainbow strips and also fold these at 2 1/2" from each end, just as you did with the first four shorter strips.

**10.** Take the two remaining 9" long rainbow strips and glue them together so that you have a piece that is 17" in length. Do not fold this strip.

**11.** Take two of the 1 1/2" x 9" pastel strips and glue them together so that you have a solid-colored piece that is 17" in length. Fold this down the center lengthwise.

**12.** Take the remaining 9" strip, which will be used for the handle, and fold it down the center lengthwise. (If you have a paper trimmer with a scoring attachment, that will make this easier.) Open the handle back up; lay it flat with the blank side up. Apply a glue stick to the entire inside of the handle and fold it back in half, pressing firmly to adhere. See Figure 26-2 for a diagram for printing, cutting, and folding.

**13.** Flatten out all the rainbow strips and lay the shorter four next to each other about 1/4" apart. Take the four

9" rainbow strips and "weave" them through the shorter strips to make the base for the basket. Do this without gluing first to be sure you have them all lined up correctly. Once you're satisfied with the layout, begin gluing the strips together wherever they lie on top of each other. The easiest way to do this is to lift a strip, place the glue stick where you want the glue, and simply twist. This leaves a small circle of glue just where you need it. Proceed with the rest of the glue joints until you have all the pieces glued together on the bottom of the basket.

**14.** Fold each piece again where you had it folded originally so that the sides of the basket are standing up. Start to feed the 17" long rainbow strip around the sides, weaving in and out as you did with the strips for the base, gluing and folding as you go. Trim off any excess when you get back to the beginning.

**15.** Take the 17" long solid pastel strip. This will be used to cap the top exposed edges of the rainbow strips. Lay the long folded strip open, blank side up, and apply glue to the entire surface. Now place it over the edges of the rainbow strips, one at a time, folding and pressing to adhere as you go around the entire edge of the basket. Again, trim any excess when you get back to the beginning.

# 27. Revolving Musical Carousel

Remember Vicky's carousel from Chapter 2? It began as the base of an empty CD spindle case—a great example of how you can put unexpected materials to use in crafts! In fact, it was a contest winner on The Crafty PC website. In this project, you'll create the carousel for yourself. By adding a small music box movement with a turntable attachment and a wonderful satin ribbon as a base cover, the carousel now becomes the perfect gift! Great for a baby shower, birthday present, or for any special occasion!

## Instructions

**1.** Open a blank page in your graphics program. Measure the diameter of the circular base of the CD spindle case. Draw a circle on your blank page in that size (usually about 5 1/2") and fill with whatever color or design you wish. Center it on the page.

**2.** Measure the diameter of the post in the center of the spindle base and add a smaller circle in that size to the center of the larger circle on your page. You will be cutting this inner circle out so the "floor" will slip over the spindle and sit on the bottom of the base (see Figure 27-1).

**3.** Print the page on card stock and cut out the large circle, cut out the smaller circle in the center, and slide the floor over the spindle. Trim as necessary to fit the base of your spindle case and glue the floor in place.

**4.** Measure the height of your center spindle and, on another blank page in your graphics program, draw a rectangle to that height and about 3" wide. Add color or art to match your flooring. Print this rectangle on card stock and cut it out. Run a line of glue (or use a glue stick) along the longer edge of one side and wrap the

## Materials

- Empty 50-CD spindle case
- Card stock
- 1/4" wired ribbon
- Polymer clay (optional)
- 1" or 1 1/4" plastic, wood, or Styrofoam ball
- Wind-up music box movement and 3" turntable
- Decorative lace trim
- Two feet of 2" wide wired ribbon (to cover base)
- Carousel horse clip art (Vicky found these on a dollhouse website.)
- Rounded toothpicks (For the horse poles—you can paint them yourself ahead of time or buy them already colored.)
- Decorative cording (optional to wrap around base of the center pole)
- Glue
- Scissors

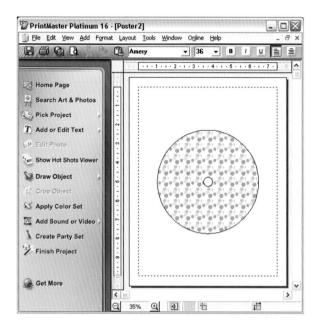

**Figure 27-1:** The floor of the carousel can be filled with any color or design you like.

rectangle into a cylinder. Once it's dry, apply a bead of glue to the inside of the bottom rim of this cylinder and slide it down over the CD spindle. The bead of glue on the inside rim should adhere the cylinder to the flooring. (Note that if you want to make your center pole sturdier, you can double up the card stock on this part.) Here's where you can add a bit more decoration—glue some decorative ribbon around the cylinder and some cording around the base of the cylinder.

**5.** On another blank page in your graphics program, place your carousel horse clip art. You will need five horses for this project, so you will be printing 10 of them. To make them all double-sided, *just remember to print one set mirrored or "flipped."* The horses should measure only slightly shorter than the center pole you glued on to your spindle case.

**6.** If you're not using the colored toothpicks for the individual horse poles, you can add poles to your graphic simply by drawing a skinny rectangle and

placing it behind your horses before you print them. If you will be using the toothpicks, you can leave that part out.

**7.** Print your horses on plain paper first to make certain the size and layout is correct. If you've done it correctly, you should have five horses facing in one direction and the other five facing the opposite way. Glue the matching pieces together and make sure the fit and layout works on your CD base before you print them out on card stock. Once you are satisfied with the horses, print them on the card stock, cut them out, glue all the matching pieces together, and allow them to dry.

NOTE **IMPORTANT!** *If you are using the toothpicks for the horse poles, glue one in between the sides of each horse before you glue the horse together! If you painted the toothpicks yourself, be sure the paint is dry before you glue them to the horses. The last thing you want to do is have paint running from inside the horse!*

**8.** Attaching the horses to the base can be done in a variety of ways. Our contest winner made small cones of polymer clay and baked them prior to gluing them to the base. (Do not bake clay on the spindle case—the case will melt!) She also added small embellishments made of polymer clay to other areas of the carousel—all baked before being applied to the spindle case. If you do not want to use polymer clay, you can make small cones out of paper, glue them to the base of the CD case, and insert the horses into them, or try small cones of Styrofoam— painted or glittered or otherwise decorated to match the rest of your design—or get out that trusty glue gun and make little mounds of hot glue and insert the horses into them. If you work quickly enough, you can even add some embellishment by sprinkling some glitter on the hot glue mounds before they totally cool. (HINT: Practice the hot glue mounding on a piece of cardboard before you attempt it on the carousel!)

# 27. Revolving Musical Carousel (cont.)

**9.** Attach pieces of your 1/4" wired ribbon to the top of each horse pole and glue the other end to the top of the plastic spindle center. The ribbon ends will be covered by the ball glued on top.

**10.** Glue your plastic, wood, or Styrofoam ball (you can paint or embellish it beforehand—how about covering it in glue and sprinkling on some glitter?) to the top of the center cylinder. Add some of the cording around the base of the ball to match the bottom of the cylinder. Embellish the ball further as you wish.

**11.** Your music box kit should include a turntable as well as the movement. Insert the turntable into the key hole in your music box movement. Center the carousel on the turntable and glue in place. Glue the 2" wired ribbon around the edge of the *underside* of the CD case bottom (almost all of them have a little ridge on the underside that's perfect for gluing this ribbon to) and then glue some decorative lace trim around the edge of the base. Trim where the ribbon meets. If you wish, you can pull the wire through on the bottom edge to bunch it up a bit more.

# 28. Glitter Embellished T-Shirt

## Materials

- T-shirt or other fabric item
- Iron-on transfer sheet
- Fabric glue
- Microfine fabric glitter
- Artist's paintbrushes in various sizes
- Fabric glue
- Scissors
- Iron
- Waxed paper (the type you use in the kitchen works fine)

*Wouldn't you love to be able to design your own t-shirt transfer and then embellish it with glitter like those professionally done shirts you see in the store? Well, you can! The heart-shaped flag design on the left was created for the September 11th anniversary and took no time at all to embellish. This technique can also be used for tote bags or other fabric items. All you need is a little patience, lots of imagination, and tons of glitter, glitter, glitter!*

## Instructions

**1.** Design the image for your t-shirt transfer using your graphics program and decide what part or parts you want to glitter. Print the image mirrored for a white or light-colored fabric (regular) transfer sheet, or un-mirrored if you're using an opaque transfer sheet.

**2.** Iron the transfer onto your shirt or other fabric item according to the manufacturer's instructions.

**3.** Once the transfer has cooled, place a piece of waxed paper inside the shirt right beneath where you will be glittering to keep any glue from passing through to the back of the item. Pick an artist's paintbrush that is the appropriate size for the area you will be glittering and begin to "paint" a small amount of the fabric glue right onto the transfer. For large areas, it's best to do this in sections so the glue does not dry before you have a chance to apply the glitter.

**4.** Sprinkle the glitter over the area you just glued. Slide your hand inside the shirt and gently tap off the excess glitter from the inside out. Any glitter that remains on the unglued portion of the transfer or the fabric itself can be gently brushed away with another, larger artist's brush or a clean, fluffy, cosmetic blush brush. Once the glitter has been tapped and brushed away, you can begin painting the glue on the next section.

**5.** Once you have the entire area glued, glittered, tapped, and brushed, gently pick the shirt up from the table and shake off the excess glitter and return it to the jar.

**6.** Lay the shirt down again and place another piece of waxed paper on top of the glittered area and gently press to make sure that all the glitter has adhered to the glue.

That's it! Most fabric glues allow you to wash an item by machine, but make certain you check the manufacturer's instructions for any special care requirements. It's best to wash the garment inside out, and you'll probably still lose a little glitter in the wash, but large amounts of missing glitter can easily be reapplied with the paint-on method.

# 29. Baby Bib Birth Announcement

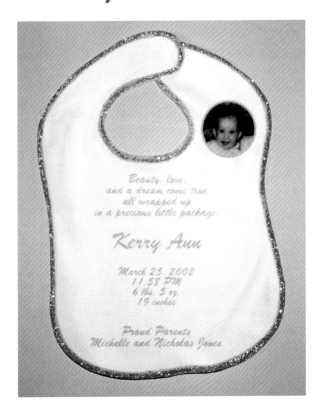

**Materials**

- Velour paper or card stock
- Glitter glue
- Baby bib photo or clip art
- Scissors
- Craft knife
- Fine artist's paintbrush
- Half-fold or print-to-the-edge envelopes
- Template 8 from Appendix C

I designed this charming and unusual birth announcement to be printed on velour paper for a wonderful texture that makes it just like a real baby bib, but you can also use inkjet fabric sheets. The edges are embellished with glitter glue applied with a fine artist's brush. The brush makes the glitter go on more evenly and allows the glue to dry quicker. I took a photo of a white satin-edged bib, changed the satin color to pink in Photoshop (you can also adjust colors in PrintMaster), added text in a coordinating color, and then added the new baby's photo for a finishing touch. The template is included in Appendix C to make it easier for you to complete this project.

**Instructions**

**1.** Scan the template into your computer and save the file.

**2.** Open a blank page in landscape orientation in your graphics program. To save on the velour paper, you'll print two announcements per page.

**3.** Place the template on the page (or use your own bib photo or clip art) and resize to fit the height of the page (watch those print margins!) Make sure the dimensions of the finished bib will fit into the envelope size you wish to use. Add text and the baby's photo as desired.

**4.** Group the bib with the text and the photo and move the grouped object to the left side of the page. Copy and paste a second bib on the right side of the page. Print a test page on plain paper.

**5.** Once you're happy with the layout, print the announcements on the velour stock. It's advisable to set your printer to greeting card paper and feed the sheets in one at a time to prevent a paper jam.

**6.** Apply a thin bead of glitter glue all the way around the colored edges of the bib and smooth out the glue with the artist's paintbrush. Set the page aside to dry for about a half-hour, and then you can cut out the bibs. Use a craft knife to cut out the neck hole.

# 30. Disposable Camera "Skin"

## Materials

- FujiFilm QuickSnap Flash disposable camera
- Inkjet paper
- Glue stick or glue
- Scissors
- Craft knife
- Cutting mat or a piece of heavy cardboard
- Template 9 from Appendix C

Crafters are always looking for new ideas for party favors. If you want your guests to remember the occasion with snapshots, try giving out disposable cameras—decorated just for the occasion. Having a wedding? How about wedding clip art or photos of the happy couple? A birthday celebration? Use photos of the guest of honor or other birthday clip art. The possibilities are endless! And don't stop with plain paper. I've made covers from holographic paper as well. You can also use foil papers, glow paper, or just about any inkjet specialty paper.

The template for this project is specifically for the FujiFilm QuickSnap Flash camera, but it can be modified to fit other FujiFilm disposable cameras as well. I picked the FujiFilm brand since the cameras were reasonably priced,

and if you want to use this item as a party favor and will be buying several of them, price will definitely be an issue.

You can also make templates for other cameras by taking the cardboard cover off, scanning it into your computer, and then "tracing" the outlines using a drawing program. Convert that tracing image into a GIF and you can design a "skin" for almost any disposable camera.

## Instructions

**1.** Scan the template into your computer and save it as a file.

**2.** Open a blank page in your graphics program in landscape orientation and insert the template into it.

**3.** Resize the template so that it measures 7 1/4" wide by 7 1/8" high. Lighten the color of the template if it's too dark.

**4.** Add your text, clip art, or photos to the white areas of the template. (The shaded areas will be cut out.)

**5.** Print a test page on plain paper. Cut it out around the outline, use your craft knife to cut out the six shaded areas, and fold on the fold and tab lines.

**6.** Remove the cardboard cover from your camera and replace it with your test "skin." If it fits well, go ahead and print it out on the paper of your choice.

**7.** Using glue or a glue stick, attach the skin to the camera.

If you prefer to fill the entire area of the skin with a design, it's not hard to do, but since the template is not transparent in the interior, it will require a few steps.

# 30. Disposable Camera "Skin" (cont.)

## Instructions

**1.** First, make sure that the template is centered on your page. Then place a rectangle over it and make certain that it extends beyond all the edges of the template beneath it. Fill this rectangle with the color or pattern of your choice and center it on the page. You should not see the template beneath it.

**2.** Print out the filled rectangle.

**3.** Go back to your project and remove the rectangle by cutting (CTRL-X)—not deleting. This enables you to paste (CTRL-V) the rectangle back in place if you need to without having to re-create it.

**4.** Now you should see only the template on your page. Flip the template horizontally, as you would for a t-shirt transfer. Put the paper with the printed rectangle back into the printer so it will print on the opposite (blank) side.

**5.** Print the template on the blank side. Cut it out and proceed as in step 4 earlier in this project.

# 31. Footed Box Greeting Card

## Materials

- Card stock (flat or glossy)
- Glue stick, craft glue, spray adhesive, or double-sided tape
- Scissors
- Bone folder or paper scorer
- Large beads for feet
- Embellishments of your choice

*This amazing little box is not only a greeting card, but it can hold a small gift as well! You can use card stock and run it through your printer to add photos and designs to the top and sides as well as to the inside, or you can use some lovely scrapbooking papers and attach them to card stock using a spray adhesive. You can add some embellishments, like little stickers adhered to the crease. But it doesn't have to be stickers! You can even print small photos and use them as well. Add some matching decorative tags on the top and bead "feet" on the bottom of the box to make this a true keepsake!*

## Instructions

**1.** Open a blank page in your graphics program in portrait orientation. Draw a rectangle that measures 8 1/2" square with a light gray outline and no fill, and center it on the page. Don't worry about part of the rectangle being outside the printable margins. The parts you need to see will be within the margins. This will be the bottom of your box. Place the lines 2 1/2 inches from the edges on all sides of the 8 1/2" square, as illustrated in Figure 31-1.

**2.** Add your designs or text as desired to the sides and inside of the box. If you're coloring the entire square, the outer edge of the box may fall outside the print margin on your inkjet, so try printing a sample on plain paper first. You'll notice on the kitten box shown at the beginning of this project that the top of the box bottom does have a white margin, but it's hidden when the top is on the box.

Total size of box bottom is 8 1/2" X 8 1/2". Dashed lines are 2 1/2" from the edges of the square. Cut out square. Cut where the red lines are shown and score and fold on all dashed lines.

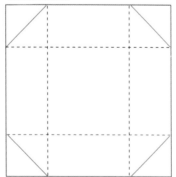

### Box Bottom Diagram

**Figure 31-1:** This is how the box bottom should look on your screen. The red diagonal lines are only for reference. You do not need to add them to your document.

# 31. Footed Box Greeting Card (cont.)

Total size of box top is 5 3/4" X 7 3/4".
Outer dashed horizontal lines are 1" from
top and bottom edges of rectangle. Inner
dashed horizontal lines are 1" from first
dashed line 2 " from edge). Vertical lines
are 1" from edge on left and right sides.
Cut rectangle on solid lines, cut out corners,
snip along red lines to inner dashed line,
and score and fold in on all dashed lines.

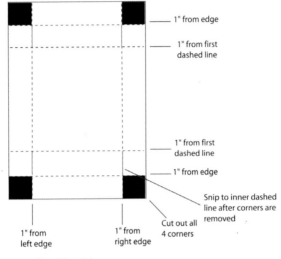

1" from edge

1" from first
dashed line

1" from first
dashed line

1" from edge

Snip to inner dashed
line after corners are
removed

Cut out all
4 corners

1" from
left edge

1" from
right edge

## Box Top Diagram

**Figure 31-2:** This is the way your box top should look on your screen. The shaded areas and the red lines are only for reference. You do not need to add them to your document.

**3.** If you want to use decorative paper on the outside of the box, glue the decorative paper to the unprinted side of the box base before cutting, scoring, and folding.

**4.** Cut out the entire square. From each corner of the card stock, cut on the red diagonal lines.

**5.** Fold inward where all the dashed lines are placed. Bring the corners of the box together, folding the paper inward.

**6.** As the paper folds together, create a crease with your fingers.

**7.** Measure and score 1 inch on all sides of the 5 3/4" x 7 3/4" card stock. This is the lid. On the short (5 3/4") sides, measure and score another inch beginning from the previous 1-inch measured mark. Figure 31-2 shows all these measurements.

**8.** Open another blank page in your graphics software in portrait orientation. Draw a rectangle that measures 5 3/4" x 7 3/4", with a light gray outline and no fill. Draw horizontal lines 1" and 2" from both the top and bottom edges and vertical lines 1" from both the left and right edges of the rectangle, as illustrated in Figure 31-2. Add whatever images, text, or color fill you wish, and cut out the box top.

**9.** Fold all score measurements inward to form your lid. Cut four 1-inch squares from the corners. The creases will show the lines to cut the squares. On the short (5 3/4") sides of the lid, cut a 1-inch tab on each side.

**10.** Bring the two tabs inward on the box and tape. You will fold over the end folds and tape, creating the end of the lid. Use the same method on the opposite side of the lid. Put the box and lid together. Glue beads on the bottom corners of the box for feet.

**11.** If you like, add matching tags to the box top. You can add further embellishment by adding some small gold or silver tassels (available at your craft store) to the bottom corners of the box top for a truly elegant look!

# 32. Scratch-Off Tickets

## Materials

• Card stock (or perforated inkjet cards)

• Peel and stick scratch-off labels

• Scissors or paper trimmer (for non-perforated card stock)

Make your own scratch-off tickets! You can use them to offer promotional discounts for your own business, as grab-bag tickets for a kid's party, or secret gift "coupons" for a loved one. This project has lots of uses and is so easy to make. You can make it even simpler to design by using perforated inkjet business cards that come 10 to a sheet. Design just one and print out a sheet of 10 at a time. Then just fold and break along the perforations. All that's left to do after that is to apply the scratch-off labels!

## Instructions

**1.** Open a blank page in your graphics program and draw a rectangle the size you wish to make the card. If you're using perforated inkjet card sheets (for business cards, postcards, raffle tickets, etc.), select that new project in your program.

**2.** Design your ticket with the text and clip art of your choice. Adjust for size and placement until you are satisfied with the layout (see Figure 32-1).

**3.** Place a circle somewhere on the card, approximately 1" in diameter. (Most scratch-off labels are circular and come in sizes ranging from 1" to 1 1/4", but you may wish to use full sheets of scratch-off labels to cut the label to any size or shape you prefer. See Appendix B, "Resources: Where to Find It," for information on where to find scratch-off labels.) Place your hidden message inside this circle.

NOTE If you wish to print a colored background on your cards, be sure to leave the inside of the circle either white or a very light color so that the hidden message can be seen easily when the label is scratched off.

**4.** Print a sample on plain paper to make sure your layout and sizing is correct. Once you're satisfied, you can print your cards or tickets on card stock.

**5.** Peel the scratch-off labels from their backing sheet and apply them on top of the circle containing your hidden message.

**Figure 32-1:** A scratch-off ticket done as a business card project. The scratch-off label will be placed over the circle that says "15%",

# 33. Fabric Gift Bag

Using any cotton broadcloth-type fabric cut to size and prepped for an inkjet printer, or using inkjet fabric sheets, you can print a design, a photo, or a special message and make a gift bag that will be as treasured as the gift inside. And to make it even better, it's easy to make this bag without having to do any sewing at all. You can even make the bag twice the size by using two fabric sheets and sewing them together!

## Instructions

**1.** Open a blank page in your graphics program in landscape orientation.

**2.** Place a straight line from top to bottom and center it so that the page is divided in half. This line will be removed once your design is set and you've printed out your test page.

NOTE *If you're using an inkjet fabric sheet, you can skip the next step.*

**3.** Prepare the fabric for the printer either by spraying it with spray starch and ironing it until it is just stiff enough to feed through the printer (make sure you trim off any frayed threads from the edges) or by ironing a piece of freezer paper to the back of the fabric to serve as a fabric carrier. This will be peeled off after the printing is complete.

**4.** On your blank page, design your bag with clip art, photos, or text, as you desire.

## Materials

• Inkjet fabric or a piece of cotton broadcloth cut to 8 1/2" x 11"

• Fabric glue, hot glue, or an iron-on fusible webbing tape

• Needle and thread or sewing machine—if you decide to sew the bag

• Self-adhesive hook and loop "dots"

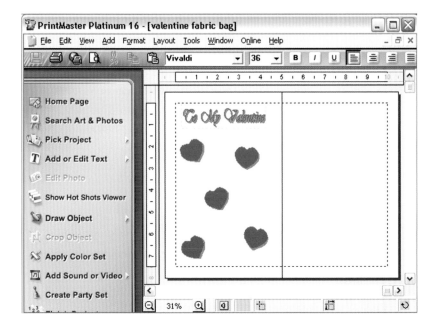

**Figure 33-1:** This is how your layout should look, leaving enough room around the edges of the front of the bag for a 1/2" seam allowance.

**5.** If the design is the same on the front and back of your bag, you can do the design on one side of the dividing line you placed on the page, and then group, copy, and paste to the other side. Just make sure you leave yourself about a half-inch all the way around the design to allow for seams (see Figure 33-1).

**6.** Once the design is finished, print a test page out on plain paper and fold at the dividing line to make sure alignment is correct and that there is enough of a seam allowance.

**7.** Once you're satisfied with the layout and alignment, delete the dividing line from the page and print the design out on the prepared fabric or inkjet fabric sheet. If you went the freezer paper route, peel that off the fabric.

**8.** Either sew a tiny hem along the top of the bag or use fabric glue, a hot glue gun, or the iron-on fusible webbing tape to do this.

**9.** Once the top hem is finished, fold the fabric sheet in half with the unprinted sides facing you. Now you can either sew the sides and bottom seam or use the glue or fusible webbing tape to do the same. Trim all seams to about 5/8" after they are sewn or otherwise fused. Turn the bag right side out.

**10.** Cut each part of a hook and loop dot in half and stick them to the inside of the top of the bag to serve as a closure.

# 34. Table Tent

This table tent matches the *Wedding Heart Rice Bag*. It's a great idea if you want to coordinate a design for a particular event or occasion. It can be used for place cards, or you can design it with a photo of the special guest(s) and put one or two on each table to commemorate the special day.

## Materials

• 110 lb. card stock (or the heaviest your printer will handle)

• Scissors or paper trimmer

• Blank business cards (an optional time-saver)

• Glue stick

## Instructions

**1.** Open a blank page in your graphics program in portrait orientation. Draw a rectangle that measures 4 1/4" wide by 7 1/2" high with no fill (or fill it with the color of your choice if you want to match the décor) and a light gray outline. Center this rectangle on the page. Save the file.

**2.** Draw a smaller rectangle that measures 3" x 13/16" (or .83 inches), also with no fill and a light gray outline. Place this rectangle at the top of the larger rectangle so that half of it is above the larger rectangle outline and half of it is below. Center this rectangle horizontally only.

**3.** Copy, paste, and move the second smaller rectangle to the bottom edge of the larger rectangle. Place it the same way you did the one on the top and also center it horizontally, as shown in Figure 34-1. These smaller rectangles are the parts you cut out to make the "legs" on your table tent.

**4.** Draw a horizontal line in the same gray as your rectangle outlines and center it on the page. This will be the fold line for your table tent.

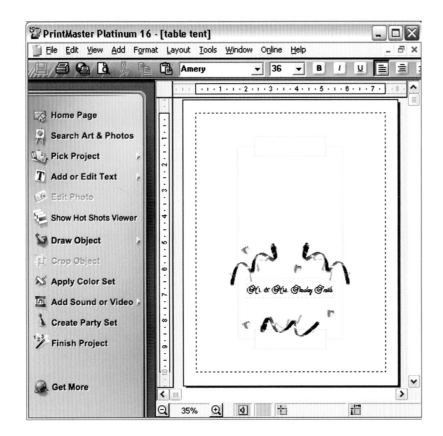

**Figure 34-1:** This is how the table tent should look on your screen. You may choose to add different clip art.

**5.** Group the line and all the rectangles and save the file once again.

**6.** Now you can add your clip art and text. The bottom portion of the page will be the front of the table tent, so make sure this is the half on which you place your text.

**7.** Save the file. Print it out on card stock and cut it out. Don't forget to cut around the smaller rectangles to make those "legs."

**8.** Fold the table tent at the center line.

**9.** Take a blank business card (or cut a piece of card stock 2" x 3 1/5"). Fold lengthwise about 1/4" in from each edge. Apply glue to the folded edges and place the business card inside the bottom of the table tent. Center it as best you can and press to adhere to the front and back of the table tent. This will stabilize the tent so it won't "lie down on the job" halfway through your event!

# 35. Votive Candle Column

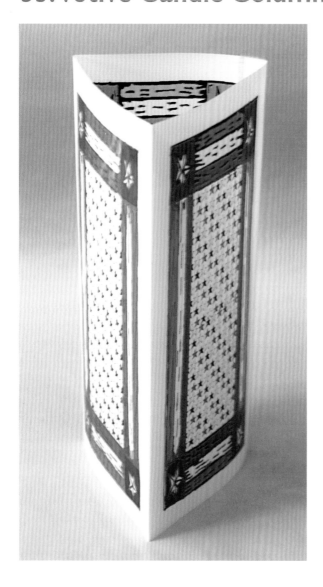

This easy project is made from backlight film and slips over any glass votive holder up to 2 inches wide. It's a simple way to dress up the table, or place them anywhere in your yard for some special ambience!

NOTE Backlight film is flammable, so be careful!

**Instructions**

**1.** Open a blank page in your graphics program in landscape orientation.

**2.** Draw a straight line from the top of the page to the bottom and give it a light gray outline. This will serve as one of your folding lines. Make two copies of this line and place them so that the page is divided into three 3.5" sections. There will be a 1/2" section left at the end that will be the flap.

NOTE It's easier for printing purposes if you place the flap on the left side of the page on your screen. Those print margins again!

**3.** Place your clip art into one of the three sections and resize it so that it hits the top and bottom margins.

**4.** Copy your design twice and place the two copies into the two remaining sections, as shown in Figure 35-1.

**Materials**

• Backlight film

• Double-sided tape

• Votive candle in glass holder (up to 2" wide)

• Clip art

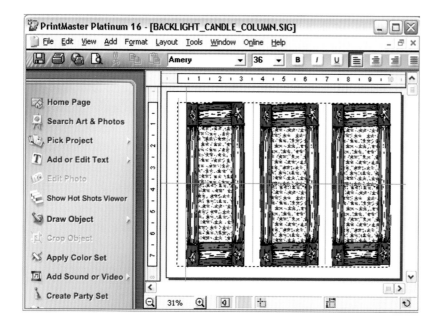

**Figure 35-1:** Once you have copied and pasted your design, this is what it should look like on your screen.

**5.** Print a test page on plain paper. Fold on all lines to check placement. If you're happy with the printout, print your candle column on the *dull* side of a sheet of backlight film.

**6.** Allow the ink to dry for a minute or two. Score and fold on the gray lines. Be careful when scoring if you're using a scoring blade; too much pressure will cut through the backlight film.

**7.** Place double-stick tape on the inside of the edge opposite the flap (it's easier than placing the tape on the flap itself) and press the flap into place on the tape.

# 36. Pop-up Sleeve Holiday Card

The front of the card holds the first part of your holiday message. When the recipient slides the sleeve down, a surprise awaits them! A separate piece of clip art with the rest of your message! When opened, the card stands like a tent card. Your friends and family will be amazed at your craftiness with this one. Each card uses three sheets of card stock, and with the template supplied, all you have to do is follow the instructions, and you'll produce a creative greeting card. All measurements are provided to make this card fit into a standard bi-fold greeting card envelope. There may be a lot of steps to this card, but the results are well worth the effort.

## Instructions

**1.** Open a blank page in your graphics program in portrait orientation. Scan the template for the card and save the file.

**2.** Import the template into your blank page and resize it so that it measures exactly 5 1/2" wide by 10" high. This is important to ensure that the finished card will fit into a bi-fold envelope.

**3.** Center the template on the page and save the file. The two gray horizontal lines in the lower part of the template are your fold lines, so make sure you can always see them. This means making certain that the template is always in front of any graphics, so they will show when you print the card (see Figure 36-1).

**4.** Select a background clip art appropriate for the holiday or occasion for which you're creating this card. Fit it to the template in height and width, but not all the way up into the two little tabs at the top—these are also for folding. You can also draw a rectangle to fit these dimensions and fill it with the color or texture of your choice instead of using a clip-art background.

## Materials

• 110 lb. card stock (or the heaviest your printer will handle)

• Scissors

• Paper trimmer (optional, but a real time-saver!)

• Glue stick or double-stick tape

• Holiday clip art

• Template 10 from Appendix C

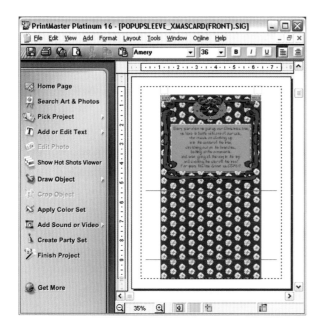

**Figure 36-1:** The gray horizontal lines show where the card will be folded. Make sure they are always visible and in front of your design (the top layer).

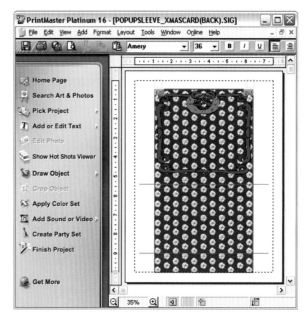

**Figure 36-2:** The back of your card looks exactly the same as the front, except the text box has been removed.

**5.** If you wish to add an additional clip-art design like the ribbon and wreath border we used, do so now, but make certain it's placed above that first gray folding line. Center this clip art horizontally on the page and save the file again. (Refer to Figure 36-1.)

**6.** Now add a text box and fill it with color, if you choose. Add the text for the front of your card and save the file one more time.

**7.** If you like, you can do what we did and add a tiny text box in the top right and top left corners with the words "Slide Down," so your recipient knows what to do to see the inside of the card.

**8.** Print a test page on plain paper and check to make certain the measurements—including the little tabs at the top—match the measurements we gave you earlier.

**9.** If all looks good, print the front of the card on the card stock.

**10.** Now go back to your page and remove the text box. Save this file with a different name, like "card back," to distinguish it from the front of the card (see Figure 36-2).

**11.** Print this on card stock as well.

**12.** Now it's time to make the interior part of the card that will pop up when the recipient slides the outer sleeve down. You can choose whatever clip art you like, as long as the measurements are as follows: 4 1/2" wide by 8 1/2" high. This ensures that the interior piece will fit through the opening at the top of the sleeve and that it will not extend past the top of the card when it is closed flat. Add your text box, but make certain it's in the top half of the interior piece, because only the top half will show when the card sleeve is opened (see Figure 36-3).

# 36. Pop-up Sleeve Holiday Card (cont.)

**Figure 36-3:** The tree will be the part that pops out of the card when you slide the outside down. This tree measures 4.45" wide and 8.45" high.

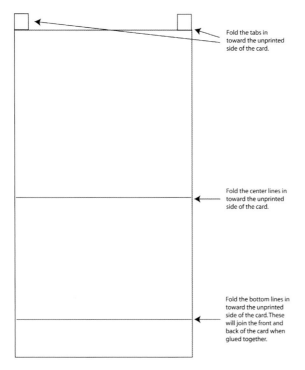

Fold the tabs in toward the unprinted side of the card.

Fold the center lines in toward the unprinted side of the card.

Fold the bottom lines in toward the unprinted side of the card. These will join the front and back of the card when glued together.

**Figure 36-4:** Where and how to fold the front and back pieces of the card

**13.** Print a test page on plain paper and check the sizing. Once you're satisfied, save this file and print it on a piece of card stock.

**14.** Now comes the fun part! Cut the front and back out using a paper trimmer or scissors, being careful not to snip off the little tabs at the top.

**15.** Fold the two fold lines on both the front and back of the card. Make sure you fold them in toward the unprinted side of the card.

**16.** Fold the small tabs at the top—also toward the unprinted side of the card front and back, as shown in Figure 36-4.

**17.** Cut out your interior piece and, with the bottom of the card back folded, place your interior piece on top of it to make certain there is nothing extending beyond the top of the card. If there is, trim a bit off the bottom of your interior piece.

**18.** Once the fit of the interior and exterior parts of the card is satisfactory, lay the card back—printed side down—on the table, with the bottom flap folded up. If you've done this correctly, the only printed part you should see is the lower flap.

**19.** Glue the bottom of your interior piece to this flap with the printed side up, making sure it is centered and not extending past the top of the card. (You can also use double-stick tape for all the adhering.)

**20.** Glue or tape the printed side of the bottom flap on the front of the card. Press the front and back flaps of the card together so that the bottom flaps are adhered.

Both small tabs should be folded down toward the unprinted side of the card. Also fold the tabs on the front of the card toward the unprinted side. Glue the tabs on the card back to the corresponding tabs on the card front. ONLY the tabs should be glued together.

Back of card with printed side down.

Glue the base of the pop-up piece to the printed side of the lower flap on the card back.

Fold lower flap up so the printed side faces you (do this on card front *and* card back.)

After the pop-up piece is glued in place, fold up the lower flap of the card front and glue to the flap on the card back. ONLY the flaps will be glued together.

**Figure 36-5:** How to assemble the card

**21.** Now glue the front surface of the small tabs at the top of the card front. Fold them in; fold in the top tabs on the back of the card and press to adhere the tabs to one another, as shown in Figure 36-5.

**22.** Now for the action part! Slide the top of the card down until the bottom of the card is flat. (The other set of fold lines will do the job here.) You'll see the top half of the interior part of the card rise up from within the card, and the second part of your message will be revealed!

# 37. Mother's Day Bath Basket

Make a special handmade gift basket filled with bath products so Mom can pamper herself a little. This basket contains bath oil, after-bath splash, bath salts, a scented candle, two hand towels and washcloths color-coordinated to Mom's bath, and a few sea shells thrown in for special effect. The labels have fancy text on them that state what the product is—Mom's Bath Oil, Mom's Bath Salts, Mom's Candle, and so on. I added some seashell clip art to tie it all together and a gift tag with the same clip art and fancy text. The fancy corked bottles can be purchased at your local craft store, as well as the sea shells, the candle, the basket, and the tulle; you can also use a sheer ribbon for the same effect.

The labels on the bottles are made using waterproof glossy adhesive-backed paper. The same paper is used for the candle, since I opted to place the label over the cellophane wrapping on the candle so that it would keep its fragrance longer, but you may decide you would rather place the candle in the basket without the cellophane wrapper. In that case, use a white waterslip decal and apply it directly to the candle. The envelope containing the bath salts is made from plain inkjet paper and put together with either a glue stick or double-stick tape.

It's an easy project to make. The only other items you need to purchase are the towels and the bath products in your Mom's favorite scent! You can even wrap the finished basket in decorative cellophane, or go all out and buy some shrink wrap from your craft store. Wrap the basket in the shrink-wrap. Use a blow dryer to heat and shrink it and top if off with a big, beautiful bow!

## Materials

- Basket
- Hand towels and washcloths
- Decorative bottles
- Scented candle
- Various seashells
- Bath oil or bubble bath
- After-bath splash
- Bath salts or beads
- Tulle "by the yard" or sheer ribbon
- Waterproof glossy adhesive-backed paper
- Waterslip decals (optional for the candle)
- Card stock (for the gift tag)
- Plain inkjet paper (for the bath salts envelope)
- Single-hole punch
- Scissors
- Glue stick or double stick tape
- Cellophane or shrink-wrap (optional)

## Instructions

**1.** Measure the faces of the decorative bottles to get the dimensions for your labels. Open a blank page in your graphics program and draw the shape you need to outline the labels. These shapes should have no fill and a very light gray outline. Add your text and clip art as desired—you can even add a photo of Mom to the labels! If you'll be placing your candle label on the cellophane wrapper, design this here as well.

**2.** Print these labels out on plain paper and cut them out to check the size on your bottles and candle. Adjust as necessary until you get the dimensions correct and then print them out on a sheet of waterproof glossy adhesive-backed paper.

**3.** Cut the labels out and apply to cleaned surfaces on the front of your bottles and to the cellophane wrapper on the candle.

**4.** Fill the bottles with the bath oil or bubble bath and after-bath splash. (If you're using cork-topped bottles and are worried about leakage, seal the bottles by lighting a birthday candle and using the dripping wax to seal around the base of the cork and bottle top. Just be careful!)

**5.** Open another blank page in your graphics program in landscape orientation and draw a rectangle measuring 4 1/2" wide by 5 3/4" high with no fill and a light gray outline. Move this rectangle to the left side of the page.

**6.** Copy and paste this rectangle and drag it, while holding down the CTRL key, so that it lines up to the right of the first rectangle.

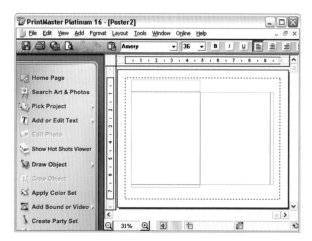

**Figure 37-1:** Layout for the bath salts envelope

**7.** Copy and paste the second rectangle; then resize it so that the height remains the same, but the width is reduced to 1/4". Again, drag while holding down the CTRL key so that this skinnier rectangle is lined up to the right of the second rectangle. This is the side tab that will be glued to the front of the envelope.

**8.** Copy and paste the first rectangle. Resize, leaving the width as is but reducing the height to 1/4". CTRL-drag this rectangle so that it lines up below the first rectangle. This is the bottom tab that will be glued.

**9.** Repeat step 6, but make the height about 3/4" to 1". CTRL-drag to the top of the first rectangle. This is the flap closure for the envelope (see Figure 37-1).

**10.** Group all the rectangles and move them so that there is little or no extension beyond your inkjet's print margins. Now place your text and clip art as you did for the labels on the left-most rectangle. (Copying and pasting from your labels page will make this go a lot quicker!)

# 37. Mother's Day Bath Basket (cont.)

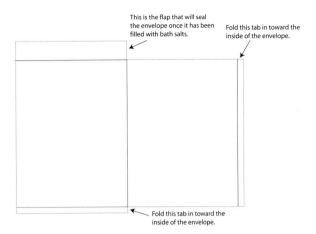

This is the flap that will seal the envelope once it has been filled with bath salts.

Fold this tab in toward the inside of the envelope.

Fold this tab in toward the inside of the envelope.

**Figure 37-2:** How to fold the tabs on the envelope

**11.** Print the envelope on plain inkjet paper and cut it out. Fold on all lines, as indicated in Figure 37-2.

**12.** Apply a glue stick or double-stick tape to the two tabs and press them into place. Fold the flap over the top of the envelope. (You can also use a Post-it-type glue stick for the flap of the envelope, or you can simply close it with a small piece of scotch tape.) Fill this envelope with the bath salts or beads.

**13.** Open another blank page in your graphics program and draw a rectangle 2 1/2" x 3" (or use inkjet business cards), again with no fill and a light gray outline. This will be your gift tag. Use the same text type and clip art as on your labels. Print on card stock and punch a hole in one corner to tie a piece of ribbon through to attach the card to the basket.

**14.** If you have decided to make the candle with a

waterslip decal, open another page, design your candle label, and print it on decal paper.

**15.** Now it's time to put it all together. First, weave your tulle or ribbon through the basket as desired. Then roll the two hand towels and place them in the bottom of the basket. Do the same with the washcloths, stuffing them into the front of the basket. They will serve as the "stage" for the bottles, candle, and envelope. Then line up the bottles, candle, and envelope, add the seashell accents, attach your gift card, and stand back for a minute to admire your handiwork. Finish up the project by wrapping the whole basket with cellophane or shrink-wrap, add that big bow, and Mom has a gift that she will treasure! And she'll think of you every time she sinks into that warm tub and lights that deliciously scented candle!

# 38. White Waterproof Window Clings

**Materials**

• Inkjet window cling sheets

• Waterproof glossy adhesive-backed inkjet paper

• Scissors

• Clip art

Think you can't make white waterproof window clings on an inkjet printer? Think again! With some regular clear ink-jet window clings and waterproof glossy adhesive-backed inkjet paper, it's a breeze! Just think of all the personalized window clings you can make. Having a party for a graduate in your house? Want to celebrate Father's Day, Flag Day, or the Fourth of July in decorative style? Make your own window clings that can be applied to the outside of your windows.

**Instructions**

**1.** Open a blank page in your graphics program. Select the clip art or design whatever images you want on your window clings. Save the file.

**2.** Print your designs on the waterproof glossy adhesive-backed inkjet paper and let them dry for a few minutes.

**3.** Peel the backing off the waterproof paper and lay it flat in front of you, sticky side up.

**4.** Take the cling sheet and with the peel-off side facing you, line it up with the bottom of the waterproof paper. *Slowly* begin to adhere the cling sheet to the waterproof paper a little at a time to avoid any bunching or bubbling.

**5.** Press with your hand across the entire sheet to adhere it well.

**6.** Cut out your designs, cutting through all the layers.

**7.** I advise placing the decals under a heavy book overnight to make certain they remain flat, since the heavier weight of the waterproof paper can cause some minor curling after you have cut out the designs.

**8.** When you're ready to apply the decals, make certain your window is clean in the area to which you will be applying the decals. Any dirt or dust can decrease the clinging power of the decals.

**9.** Peel the backing off the cling sheet and apply the decals to the window.

**10.** To save the decals after you remove them, place them on a sheet of baking parchment or a silicon release sheet (like the backing on a sheet of labels). Place a sheet of plain paper on top of them and store them with some weight on top of them so they stay flat. You may also place them in a large zip-lock bag, making sure they are not overlapping, and place them under some books or magazines.

# 39. Coloring Book Greeting Card

## Instructions

**1.** Open a blank half-fold greeting card in vertical orientation in your graphics program.

**2.** Design the front and inside of the card with graphics and text as desired.

**3.** Save the file.

**4.** Open another half-fold greeting card in vertical orientation. This is the one you'll use for the outlined graphics.

**5.** Select the graphic to be outlined and place it on the page. For this step, the way you do this depends on your software:

∑• If you're using PrintMaster, click on the graphics button. Set the picture type to CGM—these are the only graphics in this program that will print in outline. Select the graphic you want and place it on the first page of the coloring book.

∑• If you're using Print Artist, select any graphic and place it on the page. Then select that graphic and click on Object on the menu bar and select Color Effects. A new window opens with a scroll list of color options. First, try black and white. If there is more black in the graphic than you would like, then try using white instead of black and white. Each time you make a color selection in Print Artist, the result will be previewed on your document.

## Materials

• One sheet of half-fold greeting card stock

• One sheet of regular inkjet paper

• Long-reach stapler (available in most office supply stores) or a regular stapler

*What child wouldn't love to get an "interactive" greeting card for a holiday or for their birthday? Well, here it is! A greeting card with four pages of graphics that they can color! And why stop at four pages? As long as you have a long-reach stapler (although with a bit of effort, a regular stapler will work just as well) and a bit of imagination, this project can be turned into a coloring book with many pages!*

*The Thanksgiving card pictured uses one piece of card stock and one sheet of regular inkjet paper printed with outlined graphics on both sides. Programs like PrintMaster and Print Artist both allow you to print graphics in outline. This is a simple project that is sure to delight any child!*

**6.** Add text if you like and be sure to set the color to none or white and the outline of the letters to hairline black.

**7.** Repeat this process for the two inside sections of the card and for the back as well.

**8.** Save the file.

**9.** Print both sides of the card on the greeting card stock.

**10.** Print both sides of the coloring book portion on the regular paper.

**11.** Place the card part beneath the coloring book page and fold it in half.

**12.** Staple in the center—top and bottom—using a long-reach stapler. If you do not have one, you can use a regular stapler by "rolling" one half of the card so that it fits in the stapler and reaches the centerfold. Make sure you staple from the outside so that the prongs of the staples are on the inside of the card.

Now get ready to hand out the crayons!

# 40. Magnetic Message Board

Tired of all those little notes and pieces of paper stuck to your refrigerator? Why not make your own magnetic dry erase board to keep messages and reminders handy? No water or chemicals needed to clean this board. Simply wipe off the ink with a dry tissue. These boards can be printed to coordinate with your décor, or you can make them as gifts with special photos and designs customized for the recipient. It's a great idea for those college kids heading off to the dorm. Give it to them with a message already included—"Phone Home!!"

NOTE If you prefer not to use dry erase markers, you can use a felt tip marker made for inkjet transparencies. It will wipe off easily with a damp tissue or paper towel.

## Instructions

**1.** Open a blank page in your graphics software in portrait orientation.

**2.** Design your dry erase board with photos or clip art. (See the example in Figure 40-1.)

**3.** Print it out on card stock.

**4.** Place the card stock on the cardboard and make sure it fits correctly. You may have to trim a tiny bit off the edges of the cardboard so that it doesn't show.

**5.** Once the card stock and cardboard are the same size, apply the glue stick to the entire surface of the cardboard and place the printed card stock on top of it. Press to make certain it is well attached.

**6.** Peel the backing off the laminating sheet and place it sticky side up on the table. Carefully place the bottom edge of the card stock/cardboard onto the bottom of the laminating sheet, making certain to leave a small edge to

## Materials

• 110 lb. card stock (or the heaviest paper your printer will handle)

• 8 1/2" x 11" cardboard

• 9" x 12" peel-and-stick laminating sheet

• Glue stick

• Dry erase marker (or an inkjet transparency felt tip marker)

• White self-adhesive hook and loop "dots"

• Peel-and-stick magnetic tape

• Paper cutter/trimmer or scissors

• Clip art

Figure 40-1: An example of a board design

wrap under the back of the cardboard. Slowly lower the card stock/cardboard onto the laminating sheet a little at a time to prevent bubbling or creasing.

**7.** Cut the corners off the laminating sheet and fold the top and bottom edges of the sheet over the back edges of the cardboard. Do the same with the sides. See Figure 40-2 for an illustration.

**8.** Apply four small pieces of peel-and-stick magnetic tape to each of the four corners on the back of the board.

**9.** Turn the board over and attach a small Velcro dot (you can trim them down to a smaller size) to the right edge of the dry erase board. Put the harder part of the Velcro on the board and the softer piece on the marker.

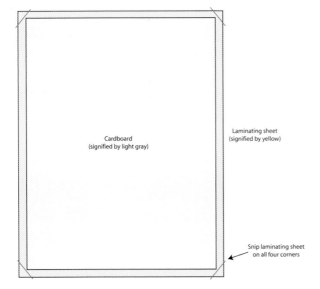

Cardboard
(signified by light gray)

Laminating sheet
(signified by yellow)

Snip laminating sheet
on all four corners

Figure 40-2: Cut the laminating sheets at all four corners before folding the edges over the cardboard.

# 41. Photo Candle

## Materials

- Candle
- Waterslip decals
- Decal finishing spray
- Scissors or paper trimmer
- Clip art

This candle makes a great gift for a decorative accessory to match the décor or as a holiday ornament. The photos are printed on waterslip decals and applied to the candle. If you use a white candle, you can use clear waterslip decals. If you choose a colored candle, be sure to use white waterslip decals, since most inkjets do not print white and any white in your photo or clip art will take on the color of the candle if you use the clear decals. These candles are great as a favor at a special party or just to add some personalized touch to your home décor.

## Instructions

**1.** Open a blank page in your graphics program in portrait orientation.

**2.** Place your photos or clip art on the top of the page. Measure the candle and size your art work accordingly.

NOTE *If you are using the white decals on a colored candle, it's easier to use a background or border that has a straight edge. Otherwise, when you cut out the finished design, you may have some white edges showing when you apply the decal to the candle. This is not a problem if you're using clear decals on a white candle, since the edges will not show when the decal is applied.*

**3.** If you're placing artwork on both sides of the candle, make certain that the two designs are the same size.

**4.** Print out a test page.

**5.** Once you're satisfied with your design and layout, print it on the waterslip decal.

**6.** Let the decal dry for a few minutes before applying two to three coats of the decals finishing spray. Always remember to apply this spray in a well-ventilated area and allow at least 30 to 60 minutes for each coat to dry.

**7.** Once the decals are thoroughly dry, cut them out. Soak them in water for approximately 20 to 30 seconds and *slowly* slide the decals off the backing sheet onto the surface of your candle. You'll have a good bit of time to reposition the decal if necessary. Blot and smooth with a soft facial tissue or paper towel.

**8.** Repeat this process with the second design if you're applying to both sides of the candle. *Be careful* when applying the second decal, because you may move the first one around without even knowing it.

**9.** Let the decals dry overnight, and you have a personalized candle that is so beautiful you may never want to burn it!

# 42. Gift Card Holder

## Materials

- Quarter-fold card stock (or any other heavyweight card stock)
- Craft knife
- Scissors or paper trimmer
- Cutting mat or heavy piece of cardboard
- Glue stick
- Clip art

If you're like me, you always have at least one or two people on your holiday shopping list for whom it's difficult to find the right gift. What do you give to the person who seems to have everything? A gift certificate! The gift certificates given by most stores these days resemble credit cards more than a certificate and usually, but not always, come with a little folder to place the card in. Well, even if they do come with the folder, why not make your own? It's an easy project and will mean so much more to the gift card recipient with your very own personalization!

Quarter-fold greeting card stock is perfect for this project, since all the scoring has already been done for you and you only print on one side. All you have to do after you design it is cut off the white unprinted margins, make a little slit for the gift card, glue it, and fold it. An instant personalized gift card holder!

## Instructions

**1.** Open a blank page in your graphics program in landscape orientation. Place a guideline from top to bottom and center it horizontally. Place another guideline from side to side and center it vertically. (These lines will not print. They are just to help you line up your clip art and text. If your software does not enable you to place unprintable guidelines, then simply draw these straight lines on your screen and remove them before printing.)

**2.** Place your clip art on the page and resize it so that it fits in one of the quadrants on the page. You can duplicate it and place the same design in every section, or make different designs for each section. That's up to you. Just make sure that the orientation is correct so that it doesn't appear upside down or backward when you fold it.

**3.** Place your text where you want it. Text for the front of the card holder will be placed in the upper-left quadrant and must be oriented so that it is upside down and backward on your screen. Text for the inside goes in the lower quadrants. No reorientation is necessary. Just make sure you have your spacing lined up according to your guidelines, as illustrated in Figure 42-1.

# 42. Gift Card Holder (cont.)

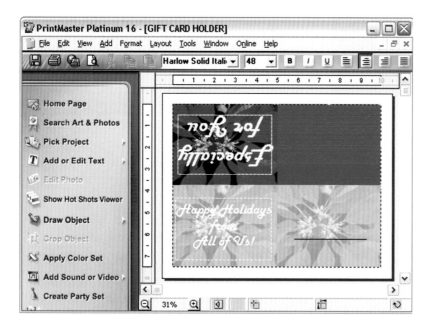

**Figure 42-1:** The layout for the gift card holder. It will be folded into quarters after it is cut out.

**4.** Place a horizontal line 3.5" long on the lower-right quadrant and center it horizontally in that quadrant. In addition, move it up or down so that it is about one-third of the way up from the bottom of the clip art. This is the line you will cut to slip the gift card through. (Refer to Figure 42-1.)

**5.** Print a test page on plain paper. If everything lines up correctly, print it out on your quarter-fold card stock.

**6.** It's advisable to fold your gift card holder before you trim away any unprintable white margins. This ensures a cleaner edge when you do trim it down.

**7.** Once you have the edges trimmed, unfold the card holder and lay it flat—printed side up—on a cutting mat or a heavy piece of cardboard. With your craft knife, cut the slit that will hold the gift card.

**8.** Turn the card holder over and spread your glue stick around all the edges. Be careful not to place too wide a glue strip underneath the slit, or you won't be able to slip the gift card in. Also, place some glue in the centers of the three quadrants that do not have the slit.

**9.** Fold the card in half lengthwise and press to adhere the glue. Slip your gift card into the slit, fold it closed, and you're done!

# 43. St. Patrick's Day Pop-Up Card

## Materials

- Card stock
- Glue or glue stick
- Double-stick tape (optional)
- Craft knife
- Cutting mat or heavy piece of cardboard
- Clip art
- Template 11 from Appendix C

*Here's a happy leprechaun who's found his pot of gold at the end of the rainbow! A pop-up piece that's cut separately from card stock allows you to make any card a pop-up. It can be resized and trimmed, so any graphic can be used on a bi-fold card, a quarter-fold card, or a print-to-the-edge card. As long as the card opens from the side, this piece can be used. Use the template in Appendix C and make pop-ups to your heart's content!*

## Instructions

**1.** Open a blank greeting card in your graphics program so that the opening is on the side. Design the outside of your card. Save the file.

**2.** Scan and import the template for the pop-up piece and place it on the inside of your card. You're only placing it here temporarily to figure out the sizing for your pop-up.

**3.** Position the pop-up piece so that the center lines up with the fold on the inside of your card. Now resize the length and width as desired (see Figure 43-1). You can trim the piece later if need be. Make note of the measurements of the pop-up piece once you have it the size you want.

**4.** Copy and paste the pop-up piece into a blank page in portrait orientation and double-check your measurements. Save this file. Now add the clip art that will be attached to the pop-up piece and make certain that the dimensions from left to right are about the same as the pop-up. The height can be higher. Place this clip art on the top half of the page. Leave the pop-up piece on the bottom half of the page.

**5.** Print the page on card stock.

**6.** Go back to your greeting card and design the inside. Leave the pop-up template in place on that document until you have finished designing the inside of the card. This allows you to make certain that your design does not interfere with the pop-up piece. Once you have the inside of the card designed, you can delete the pop-up piece from that document and print out your card.

**7.** Cut out the pop-up piece and the clip art that will be attached to it.

# 43. St. Patrick's Day Pop-Up Card (cont.)

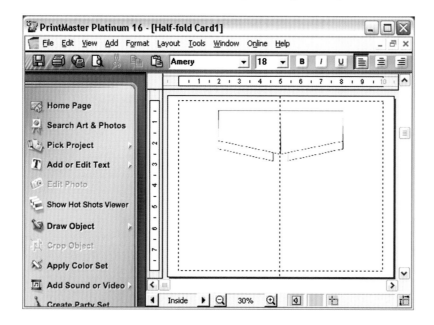

**Figure 43-1:** The inside of a half-fold card showing the pop-up piece

**8.** Fold the pop-up piece back on the center line and fold the two bottom tabs toward the back on their fold lines. Now fold your clip art in half so that the art is on the outside. Glue the clip art to the pop-up piece so that the bottom of the center folds match. Don't worry that parts of your clip art extend past the bottom of the pop-up piece—you'll be trimming this in a minute.

**9.** Once the clip art is attached to the pop-up template, fold the bottom flaps back on the template and trim any edges off your clip art so that it matches the angle on the bottom of the template. Trim the sides if necessary. If your design requires cutting elements out of the inside of the design, use your craft knife to do this now.

**10.** Open the greeting card flat on the table or desk and attach two small pieces of double-stick tape (you may have to trim it to make the pieces a little narrower) to the underside of the folded flaps on the bottom of the pop-up. Position the pop-up on the inside of your greeting card so that the center folds match up. Remember that while the fold on the card is a "valley" fold (folds inward), the fold on the pop-up piece will fold in the opposite direction.

**11.** Close the card and press it flat. If you're not satisfied with the placement of the pop-up, the double-stick tape should allow you to remove and reposition it a couple of times. Glue, on the other hand, does not allow you to reposition as easily and doesn't stick as well as the tape.

# 44. Vellum Insert Self-Mailer

## Materials

- Inkjet vellum
- High-resolution 35 lb. inkjet paper
- Scissors or paper trimmer
- Clip art

NOTE *You can use 110 lb. card stock or any other weight card stock, but I like the high-resolution paper because the colors are especially vibrant, and they show through the vellum nicely.*

*This little self-mailing invitation is printed on a high-resolution 35 lb. paper available in office supply stores and designed on both the inside and the outside with your choice of clip art and the address of the recipient. The text of the invitation is printed on a vellum paper, specially coated for use in an inkjet printer so the design on your cachet shows through. This is a truly professional-looking invitation, or you can use it for announcements or greeting cards.*

## Instructions

**1.** Open a blank page in your graphics program in landscape orientation.

**2.** Place a rectangle on the page and size it to 3 1/2" high and 4 1/2" wide with no fill and an outline of your choice.

**3.** Center this rectangle on the page. This is the area over which you will place the vellum insert.

**4.** Add clip art of your choice to fill this rectangle. Make certain it is the same dimensions. (If you're using a rectangular-shaped piece of clip art, you can do away with the rectangle you created in step 2. Just remember to size the clip art to measure 3 1/2" x 4 1/2".)

**5.** Add a triangle to the page with an outline and fill with a color or texture of your choice. Size the triangle to measure 4 1/2" wide and 2" high.

**6.** Position this triangle against the top of the rectangle clip art so that they just touch.

**7.** Duplicate this triangle, flip it upside down and position it against the bottom of the rectangle so the base just touches the bottom of the rectangle.

**8.** Duplicate this triangle again and resize it so that it measures 3 1/2" wide and 2 3/4" high. Rotate this triangle so that you can position it against the side of the rectangle. Again, make the base of the triangle just touch the side of the rectangle.

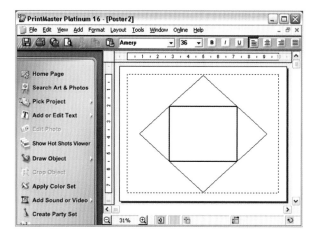

**Figure 42-1:** The layout for the gift card holder. It will be folded into quarters after it is cut out.

**9.** Duplicate this triangle, flip it horizontally, and position it on the other side of the rectangle. The result should look like Figure 42-1.

**10.** Now you need to create the front of the self-mailer. Select the entire design—all four triangles and the rectangle in the middle—and group them together. Then select the grouped design and make certain once again that it's centered on the page. Copy (don't duplicate!) the whole design.

**11.** Save your page and print it on the high-resolution paper or card stock.

**12.** Open a second page in landscape orientation and paste the first design onto that page. Center it on the page.

**13.** Ungroup and select the rectangle in the center. Delete any fill or clip art and add a text box.

**14.** Type the recipient's address into this text box and position it in the rectangular space.

**15.** Add a smaller text box for the return address, if you wish. Save the page. Create a copy for each person you invite.

**16.** Take the first page you printed and print the front of your self-mailer on the other side.

NOTE *You may find that it helps in lining the two sides up if you take the paper and turn it around so that it goes into the printer backward from the way it first came out. This allows for the differences in print margins. Experiment until you find the right placement for your printer.*

**17.** Open a third page in your graphics software. Orientation on this one does not matter. Place a text box that measures 4.5" x 3.5" and give it an outline in your choice of color and line width.

**18.** Type in the text of the invitation or announcement. Save the file and print this out on the inkjet vellum.

NOTE *Balmoral D and Vivaldi are good font choices for formal announcements, while Bernie and Andy set a more informal, fun mood.*

**19.** Allow the vellum to dry for a few minutes before you cut out the text box.

**20.** Cut out the self-mailer and trim any white edges from both sides.

**21.** Score around the rectangle on the outside—the side with the address. This prevents any of the design showing around the edges when you fold it closed.

**22.** Place your vellum piece inside the self-mailer and fold the two shorter triangles in first. Then fold in the two longer ones. Seal the self-mailer with a small adhesive seal or label.

# 45. Wedding Lights

The template for this particular shaped light cover is included the back of the book. So pull those Christmas lights out of storage, dust them off, and get ready to make a project that will have your friends and family amazed at your computer crafting savvy!

**Instructions**

**1.** Open a blank page in your graphics program in portrait orientation. Import the wedding lights template onto your page and resize it so that it measures 4.32" wide by 3.16" high. This measurement ensures that the covers are not butting up against one another when you put them on the lights, since some light strings these days have the lights fairly close together.

**2.** Place whatever clip art you choose onto the side sections of the light covers and angle the clip art so that it is aligned properly on each of the segments. Group the template and clip art, as shown in Figure 45-1.

**3.** Copy and paste the template so that you have four copies on one page.

**4.** Print one test page on plain paper. Cut out one of the templates and fold it on all lines.

**5.** Snip the point off the top of the triangle farthest away from the square tab, which is the top of the cover. This ensures that the tip of that triangle does not get in the way when you go to push the light bulb through.

**6.** Apply double-stick tape to the underside of the square tab and a small piece to the *outside* of the side tab. Now begin to attach the triangle tabs to the double-stick tape on the underside of the square tab one at a time. *Do not attach the last triangle tab that you snipped off the top!*

## Materials

- Backlight film
- Scissors
- Double-stick tape
- Single-hole punch
- String of uncolored mini-lights
- Microfine glitter (optional)
- White glue for glitter (optional)
- Small artist's paintbrush for glue application (optional)
- Holiday clip art
- Template 12 from Appendix C

These little mini-light covers were designed with wedding clip art, but they can be used for just about anything. Put any type of clip art on them that you like to match a special occasion. How about fish clip art for an outdoor summer get-together, or flags and fireworks clip art for that Fourth of July barbecue, or birthday art for a special birthday celebration? The possibilities are endless. And once you get used to using the backlight film, you can design other shapes for the light covers. Add some microfine glitter to the areas around the clip art to give it some added sparkle.

# 45. Wedding Lights (cont.)

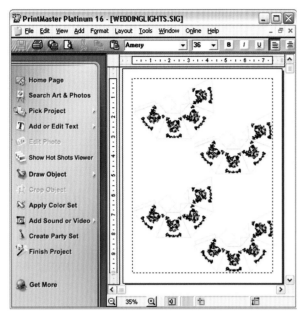

**Figure 42-1:** Angle the clip art in each section of the light template. You can fit four light covers on a page.

**7.** Holding the final side segment out of your way, punch a hole with your single-hole punch through the square tab at the top of the cover. Most single-hole punches are 1/4" and this may be a tiny bit tight for the bulbs, so we suggest that you double-punch, with the second punch slightly offset from the first to make the hole a tiny bit larger. This will make it much easier to push the bulb through from the inside of the cover.

**8.** Once you have punched the hole, you can attach the final triangle tab—the one you snipped—as well as the side tab.

**9.** Pull a bulb, complete with its holder, from the string of lights. Push the bulb and holder through the hole from the *inside* of the light cover and reinsert the bulb with the attached cover into the socket base on the light string.

**10.** If the fit is good, go ahead and print the covers on the backlight film. *Make sure you print on the dull side of the film!* The picture will show through on the clear side, which will be the outside of your light cover. Print as many as you need for the number of bulbs on your string.

**11.** Proceed as you did from step 4, making certain that you crease the folds well with your fingernail. Backlight film creases nicely if you use your fingernail. A scoring blade is not recommended for this project, as it may cut through the film.

**12.** If you're using the glitter option, apply it after you have assembled the light covers. Using the fine artist's paintbrush, apply white glue sparingly (you can dilute with water if necessary) around your clip art on all four sides of the light cover.

**13.** Sprinkle the microfine glitter over the each side and tap from the inside to remove any excess. Set each cover on a flat surface to allow the glue to set and dry thoroughly—usually about 15 minutes. Then insert the covers on the light string, as described in step 9.

# 46. Photos in Glass Ornaments

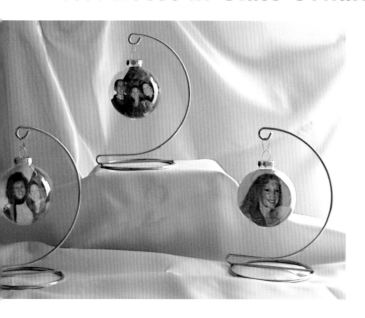

## Materials

- Clear glass ornament (about 2 1/2" in diameter)
- Ornament stand
- Backlight film
- Scissors
- Ballpoint pen or drinking straw
- Needle-nose pliers or long tweezers

A variation on the ship in a bottle, these ornaments have a flat circular photo inside them that is printed on backlight film. While getting the sizing of the photo circle can be a little tricky, inserting them into the glass ornaments is a cinch! I made several of these as Christmas gifts, and the response was always the same—"How did you do that?" If they only knew how simple it was! And the nicest thing about the backlight film is that the photo shows on both sides!

## Instructions

**1.** Open a blank page in your graphics program and draw a circle 2.63" in diameter. (This is the perfect size for the glass ornaments carried in most craft stores.)

**2.** Place your photo on the page behind the circle.

NOTE *You can skip a step by placing the photo on your page and cropping it into a circle shape and then resizing it to 2.63".*

**3.** To test how it will look placed in the glass ornament, print it on plain paper and cut out the circle.

**4.** Remove the cap and hanger from the top of the ornament. Wrap the photo circle around the barrel of the pen or drinking straw and insert it into the ornament. Once you pull the pen or straw out, the circle will open up and lie flat.

**5.** Use your pliers or tweezers to position the circle inside the ornaments where you want it. If the size and layout are satisfactory, pull the paper circle out of the ornament and print the photo circle on the dull side of the backlight film. Cut this circle out and repeat the steps described previously for inserting it into the ornament. Position it with the pliers or tweezers so that it sits in the center of the ornament.

**6.** Place the cap and loop back onto the ornament and make certain that the tails of the wire loop are positioned so that one is behind the photo and the other is in front of it. This will hold the photo circle in place and help keep it centered.

**7.** Hang your creation from an ornament stand, and you're done!

NOTE *To keep the ornament facing forward on the ornament stand as shown in the photo, add a small loop of thin wire or a large jump ring to the ornament loop before hanging it on the stand.*

# 47. Transparent Pyramid Box

## Materials

- Two inkjet transparency sheets
- Double-stick tape
- Glue stick
- Curling ribbon
- Large bead to coordinate with the color of the box
- Scissors
- Hole punch
- Gold leaf pen (optional)
- Glitter glue (optional)

*This box was designed to hold the photo ornaments shown in Project 46. The size can be altered to fit whatever object you like. Each box is made from two inkjet transparencies. Add a bead and some curling ribbon to close it; embellish with a gold leaf pen and some glitter glue, and you're all set!*

## Instructions

**1.** Open a blank page in your graphics program. Draw a square that is 4.5" x 4.5". (This size is for the ornaments in Project 46—you can make it larger or smaller depending upon what you will be placing inside.)

**2.** Fill the square with the color of your choice and move the filled square to the bottom half of the page.

**3.** Draw a triangle that is 4.5" at the base and 5.75" high. Fill it with the color of your choice. Rotate the triangle so that it fits on the page with the square.

**4.** Add a small tab at the base of the triangle by drawing a rectangle that measures 4.5" x 0.5". This rectangle should not have a fill (see Figure 47-1).

**5.** If you like, add a shape to the triangle like the star and heart and snowflake shown in the photo. Place this shape near the bottom of the triangle and make certain it has no fill. This allows the design to be clear when the sheet is printed, and you can glitter glue around the edges or use the gold leaf pen.

**6.** Group the triangle, tab, and shape design and save the file.

**7.** Select the grouped triangle and copy (CTRL-C).

**8.** Open another blank page and paste the triangle three times. Again, you will have to rotate one of the triangles so that all three will fit on the page, as shown in Figure 47-2.

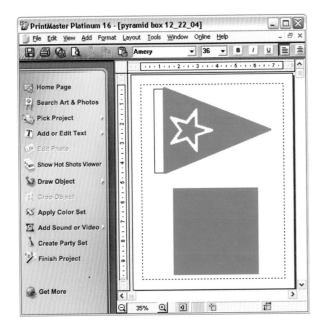

**Figure 47-1:** The base of the pyramid box and one triangular side. Print one copy of this page.

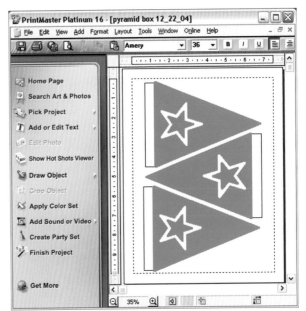

**Figure 47-2:** The three additional triangles. The center one is flipped, so all three can fit on one page.

**9.** Print both sheets on plain paper and cut out all five pieces. Fold the tabs at the base of the triangles and use a glue stick to adhere them to the edges of the square. This step is a test to make certain all the sizes are correct before you print the pieces on the transparency sheets.

**10.** Once the layout and sizes are satisfactory, print the two sheets on the rough side of the transparencies and cut out all the pieces.

**11.** Stack the four triangles together and punch a hole near the tip of the triangles. This is where you will feed through to close off the box.

**12.** Assemble the box by adding strips of double-sided tape to the outside (smooth side) of the tabs. Adhere the triangles to the inside of the square (the rough side), fold them in, and score along the edges so that the triangles will stand up.

**13.** Cut two pieces of curling ribbon approximately 18 inches in length. Feed one ribbon through two of the holes of opposite triangles. Repeat with the second piece of ribbon on the two remaining triangles.

**14.** Feed all four ribbon "tails" through the bead and move the bead all the way down to the top of the pyramid to close the box. Curl the ribbon "tails."

# 48. No-Cut CD Sleeve

**Materials**

• Any type of inkjet paper

• Photos or clip art

*Make a customized sleeve for any CD without any cutting! Just design, print, and fold. Of course, you can make this project a little extra fancy by cutting out a circle on the front of the sleeve a little smaller than the CD itself and printing on a square of inkjet transparency. Then glue that square to the inside front of the sleeve and presto—a personalized CD sleeve with a printed window on the front. This project can be printed on regular inkjet paper, but think about the possibilities if you use some fancier papers!*

**Instructions**

**1.** Open a blank page in your graphics program in portrait orientation. Draw a light gray line from top to bottom 1 3/4" from the left side. Copy and paste this line the same distance from the right side.

**2.** Draw another line from side to side and place it 4 3/4" inches from the bottom of the page. Copy and paste this line and place it 1 5/8" from the top of the page. This will be the flap. The square that results beneath the top-most line is where you will place your clip art and or text (see Figure 48-1).

**3.** Place your artwork and/or text in the center square (see Figure 48-2) and print it on plain paper to test the layout. Once printed, simply fold on all the lines. Slip your CD into the front of the envelope so that the folds are behind it. This serves to hold the flap once you've turned in the corners and folded the flap down.

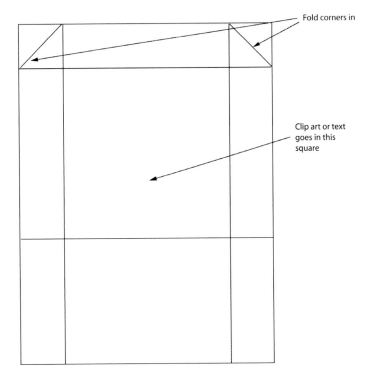

**Figure 48-1:** The layout for the CD sleeve shows where to place the clip art or text and where to fold.

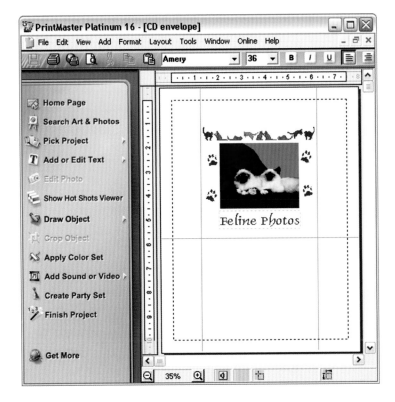

**Figure 48-2:** Your design should be placed on the upper half of the CD sleeve.

# 49. Decorative Mirror

This project was designed using white waterslip decals to make a lovely design on a regular framed mirror. The results are stunning, and it's so easy to do. Think about how you could decorate mirrors for gifts or even scan designs from your wallpaper or linens to use to pull together a bathroom or any other room in your home.

## Instructions

**1.** Open a blank page in your graphics program and use your favorite clip art to make a border. Resize your image to fit the mirror you have chosen.

**2.** Print it on plain paper and cut it out to check the sizing.

**3.** Once you're happy with your layout and sizing, print your design on a sheet of white waterslip decal paper. Let the decal dry for 15 minutes after removing it from the printer.

**4.** Spray one thin even coat of clear finishing spray. Let the decal dry for one hour, and then repeat this step again. Apply a total of three coats, letting each coat dry for an hour. Once the last coat has been applied, let the decal dry for 24 hours before cutting out your image.

**5.** If you're using a framed mirror, you need to remove the mirror from its frame. Turn the mirror over and remove any staples that are holding the mirror in place. Clean the mirror with some glass cleaner.

## Materials

- Mirror (If framed, the frame will need to be removed before the decals are applied.)

- White waterslip decal

- Decal finishing spray

- Scissors

- Craft knife

- Clip art border

NOTE *Choose an image with open spaces. This allows small sections of your mirror to show through and adds to the beauty of your mirror.*

**6.** Using a scissors or craft knife, cut out the desired areas of your design. Leave a tiny margin around the edge—about 1/8"—to prevent the ink from bleeding when the decal is soaked.

**7.** Once you have all areas cut out, place the decal into a flat bowl or pan of room temperature water. Let it soak of approximately 20 to 30 seconds, depending on the size of your decal. When the decal is ready to be applied to the mirror, it will move freely from its backing paper.

**8.** Position your decal on the desired area of your mirror and slowly slide the backing paper out from beneath the decal. Once the decal is on the mirror, you can gently reposition it. Use a soft tissue to gently dab excess water from the decal while you slowly smooth out any air bubbles. Don't worry about tiny air bubbles left behind. Most of these will disappear as the decal dries and cures. Remember to use a gentle touch to avoid tearing the decal. Let the decal cure overnight before placing the mirror back into its frame.

# 50. Matchbook Mints

## Materials

- Card stock or glossy photo paper
- Scissors or paper trimmer
- Stapler
- Candies or mints (individually wrapped)

*This little matchbook does not hold matches. It holds an individually wrapped mint or candy and makes a wonderful little gift to add to the table at a wedding or other special occasion. Add photos, text, or other images to personalize it; make it extra special by using a glossy photo paper rather than a matte card stock. They are simple to make but have a very professional look!*

## Instructions

**1.** Open a blank page in your graphics program in landscape orientation. Draw a rectangle that measures 4 1/4" high and 1 1/2" wide. Fill with your choice of color or pattern.

**2.** Place guidelines at 1 1/2" below the top, 1 7/8" below the top, and 3 3/4" from the top. These guidelines show you where you will need to score and fold the matchbook.

**3.** Place your text or images on the front and back of the matchbook using the layout diagram shown in Figure 50-1.

**4.** In order to make certain the layout and size is correct, print it on plain paper and cut it out. Score and fold at the points described in Figure 50-1. Insert the bottom of the cellophane-wrapped candy or mint into the bottom flap of the matchbook and staple it in place. Make sure the top flap closes properly. If it does not close neatly, you may have to place the staple a bit lower on the bottom flap.

**5.** Once you have the size and scoring correct, paste multiple copies on the page (as shown in Figure 50-2), print it on card stock or glossy photo paper, and proceed as above—cutting, scoring, folding, and stapling the candy into place.

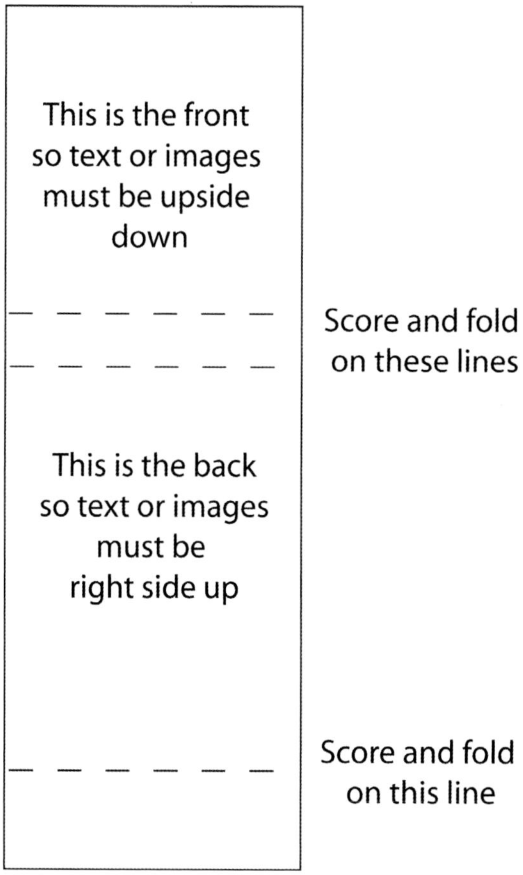

This is the front
so text or images
must be upside
down

— — — — — —
— — — — — —

Score and fold
on these lines

This is the back
so text or images
must be
right side up

— — — — — —

Score and fold
on this line

**Figure 50-1:** The layout for the matchbook mint shows the lines for scoring and folding, as well as for the placement of text and images.

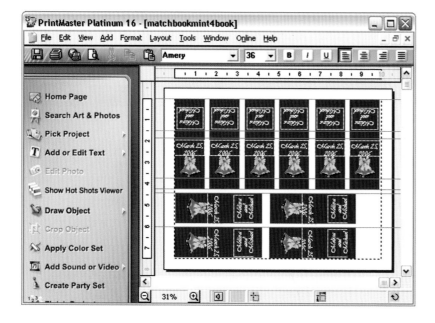

**Figure 50-2:** If you copy and paste, you can fit up to 10 matchbooks on one page.

# Appendix A

## Computer Crafting Websites and Message Boards

### Websites

This list describes some of the numerous websites out there geared toward the computer crafter:

• **www.printablepassions.com**: Printable Passions has an awesome site that offers some amazing templates for projects you can make with your computer. Most of the templates are not free, but they represent a wide variety of projects and the template prices are very reasonable.

• **www.MaggieMadeIt.com**: This site includes many computer crafting projects available at no charge.

• **www.creativegiftgiver.com/comp_gift2.htm**: The Creative Gift Giver is a great site for the computer crafter especially interested in making gifts.

• **desktoppub.about.com/od/craftideas/index. html**: This site provides links to more computer craft ideas and projects such as holiday crafts, family crafts, and birthday games.

• **www.allcrafts.net/computer.htm**: This terrific site offers lots of free computer crafting projects as well as a list of great books on computer crafting.

• **www.creativity-portal.com/howto/artscrafts/ computer.crafts.shtml**: The Creativity Portal site provides links to various computer crafting websites.

• **www.thecraftypc.com**: The Crafty PC offers instructions for dozens and dozens of free projects as well as the supplies to make them. This site also includes sections on Tips and Tricks, The Basics, Kid's Korner, and a Crafter's Gallery where computer crafters' projects are posted. The Crafty PC also runs computer crafting contests.

Looking for sites geared toward computer crafts for kids? They're out there as well! Visit some of these sites:

• **www.free-printables.com**: This site has lots of computer craft projects for children.

• **www.kidsdomain.com/craft/_computer.html**: This is another site that offers great computer crafting projects for children.

• **Cybersleuth-kids.com/Recreation/ Arts_and_Crafts/Computer_Crafts/index.htm**: This site contains links to sites that offer computer crafts for kids.

• **www.makingfriends.com/f_Friends.htm**: This site allows kids to print out paper dolls with all the necessary accessories like hair and clothing. They're great for printing on magnetic inkjet sheets. Use a cookie sheet as the base, and this makes a wonderful take-along toy to keep children happy during long car rides!

• **www.dltk-kids.com**: This site has a wealth of printable crafts for kids. They have printable greeting cards, animal crafts, holiday crafts, and crafts for specific countries and cultures.

If you're looking for websites that will help you to hone your computer skills while you craft, check these out:

• **www.creativehomecomputing.com**: Creative Home Computing provides help and resources that allow you to use your computer with confidence and creativity. In addition to providing a "Computer Challenge" and computer tips, this website also offers several project ideas.

• **www.hgtv.com**: One of my all-time favorites! On this site you'll find every project from just about every episode of the Carol Duvall Show. Even Carol has gotten into the computer crafting craze! There are at least two segments devoted to learning about computer crafting: Computing 101 and Computer Crafting. Both are on episode CDS-342. Just navigate to the Carol Duvall Show on HGTV's website and in the search box, enter that episode number, and you can read the text from that episode.

## Message Boards

Message boards and forums provide a way for you to communicate with fellow computer crafters and get great ideas for new projects. If you find yourself facing a problem trying to complete a particular craft, chances are someone on one of these boards will be able to help you.

While some message boards require you to join as a member, others are open to anyone who cares to pay a visit, read the messages, or post their own messages. These message boards are very simple to use. Just type in the web addresses shown in the following list and look for the link to the message postings—you'll find a wealth of info posted by other crafters. If you have a question or need suggestions or help with a particular project, these message boards are a great place to start!

• **www.allcrafts.net/forums/default.asp**: This is a free crafting forum and message board that includes every type of craft out there.

• **www.groups.yahoo.com/group/Computer_Crafts**: This is a board where you can share templates, websites, and help with your graphics program.

• www.groups.yahoo.com/group/ComputerGifts-Crafts: This group is for the exchange of simple and easy gifts and crafts made in part or all by computer.

• **www.groups.yahoo.com/group/Cards-n-Crafts**: This group is geared toward making cards—either

computer generated or handcrafted—and assorted crafts. This is a family-friendly group.

• **www.groups.yahoo.com/groups/Scrapbooking_ on_the_computer**: This group offers not only tips on computer scrapbooking, but on computer crafting in general.

• **www.groups.yahoo.com/group/craft_ connection**: Members of this group exchange patterns, computer crafts, and templates; post projects; and advertise their craft-related items for sale.

• **www.groups.yahoo.com/group/ computercraftingswappers**: This group offers card swaps and everything to do with computer crafts.

• **www.groups.yahoo.com/groups/0-HolidayPuterCrafts**: This group deals with all types of computer crafts. New members are accepted by referral only.

• **www.thecraftypc.com/ourmebo.html**: This message board provides tips and tricks for computer crafting and hosts an annual computer crafting contest.

• **groups.msn.com/CreativeComputerCrafts/ home.htm**: This group discusses everything related to computer crafts.

• **groups.msn.com/HarmonyHouseCreations bySusan/home.htm**: This group is primarily devoted to computer crafting using graphics from the PCCrafters Hugware collection, but its members share information about many different topics of interest to computer crafters.

# Appendix B

## Resources: Where to Find Hardware, Software, and Computer Crafting Supplies

### Hardware

**Apple**
1 Infinite Loop
Cupertino, CA 95014
(800) 676-2775
(408) 996-1010
http://www.apple.com
Computers, printers, and media

**BestBuy**
P.O. Box 949
Minneapolis, MN 55440
(888) BEST-BUY (1-888-237-8289)
http://www.bestbuy.com
Electronic superstore chain: Computers, printers, scanners, digital cameras, media, and software

**Canon U.S.A., Inc.**
One Canon Plaza
Lake Success, NY 11042
(516) 328-5000
http://www.usa.canon.com
Printers, digital cameras, scanners, and media

**CompUSA**
14951 N. Dallas Pkwy
Dallas, TX 75240
(800) 266-7872
http://www.compusa.com
Computer superstore chain

**Dell, Inc.**
One Dell Way
Round Rock, TX 78682
(800) 999-3355
http://www.dell.com
Computers and printers

**Epson America, Inc.**
3840 Kilroy Airport Way
Long Beach, CA 90806
(562) 981-3840
(800) 922-8911
http://www.epson.com
Inkjet printers and media

**Hewlett-Packard Company**
3000 Hanover Street
Palo Alto, CA 94304
(650) 857-1501
(800) 752-0900
http://www.hp.com
Computers, printers, scanners, digital cameras, and media

**Lexmark International, Inc.**
740 New Circle Road NW
Lexington, KY 40550
(800) 332-4120
http://www.lexmark.com
Inkjet printers and media

## Software

**Adobe Systems Incorporated**
345 Park Avenue
San Jose, CA 95110
(800) 833-6687
(408) 536-6000
http://www.adobe.com
Adobe Photoshop Elements 3.0, Adobe Photoshop CS2, and Adobe Illustrator CS2

**Corel Corporation**
1600 Carling Avenue
Ottawa, Ontario
Canada K1Z 8R7
(800) 772-6735
http://www.corel.com
Paint Shop Pro and CorelDRAW

**Serif, Inc.**
13 Columbia Drive, Suite 5
Amherst, NH 03031
(800) 557-3743
http://www.freeserifsoftware.com
Free software: PagePlus SE, PhotoPlus 6.0, WebPlus 6.0, DrawPlus 4.0, and 3D Plus 2.0

**Riverdeep, Inc.**
**Broderbund**
100 Pine Street, Suite 1900
San Francisco, CA 94111
(415) 659-2000
(800) 395-0277
http://www.broderbund.com
PrintMaster, Print Shop, ClickArt, ClickArt Fonts, and Scrapbook Designer

## Specialty Inkjet Media and Crafting Supplies

**A.C. Moore**
http://www.acmoore.com
Crafting superstore chain in the eastern U.S.

**ArcaMagica**
http://www.arcamagica.com
Hundreds of downloadable templates for gift boxes

**Avery Dennison**
50 Pointe Drive
Brea, CA 92821
(800) 462-8739
http://www.avery.com
Media and software

**Baudville, Inc**
5380 52nd Street SE
Grand Rapids, MI 49506
(800) 728-0888
http://www.baudville.com
Desktop publishing papers and supplies

**The Crafty PC, LLC**
1075 Easton Avenue, #308
Somerset, NJ 08873
(732) 873-8055
http://www.thecraftypc.com
Specialty inkjet media, computer crafting supplies, and free projects

**Desktop Publishing Supplies**
425 Washington Avenue
North Haven, CT 06473
(800) 443-3645
http://www.desktopsupplies.com
Inkjet papers, cards, invitations, computer crafting supplies, and more

**Eystad's Desktop Publishing Supplies**

334 S. Broadway

Pitman, NJ 08071

(888) 741-3377

http://www.edps.com

Desktop publishing and computer crafting supplies

**Hobby Lobby Stores, Inc.**

7707 SW 44 Street

Oklahoma City, OK 73179

http://www.hobbylobby.com

Crafting superstore chain

**Imaging Alternatives, Inc.**

16283 425th Street

Derby, IA 50068

(641) 533-2103

http://www.imagingalternatives.com

Inkjet printable wood veneer

**Jam Paper**

15 Hudson Avenue

Tenafly, NJ 07670

(201) 567-6666

http://www.jampaper.com

Specialty papers and envelopes

**Michael's**

http://www.michaels.com

Crafting superstore chain—nationwide and in Canada

**MicroFormat, Inc.**

830-3 Seton Ct.

Wheeling, IL 60090

(800) 333-0549

http://www.paper-paper.com

Specialty inkjet media

**Office Depot**

2200 Old Germantown Road

Delray Beach, FL 33445

(800) 463-3768

http://www.officedepot.com

Office supply superstore chain

**Paper Direct, Inc.**

100 Plaza Drive

Secaucus, NJ 07094

(800) 272-7377

http://www.paperdirect.com

Desktop publishing papers and supplies

**PhotoFrost**

21029 NE Hwy 27

Williston, FL 32692

(352) 528-9292

http://www.computercakes.com

Printable frosting sheets and edible inks

**RPL Supplies, Inc.**

280 Midland Avenue, Bldg. K

Saddle Brook, NJ 07663

(800) 524-0914

http://www.rplsupplies.com

**Transfer supplies**

Transfer Technology

A Division of BRN Corporation

3279 US Rte. 3

Thornton, NH 03223

(800) 639-3111

http://www.transfertechnology.com

Transfer supplies

# Appendix C: Templates

## Purse Favor Bag Template

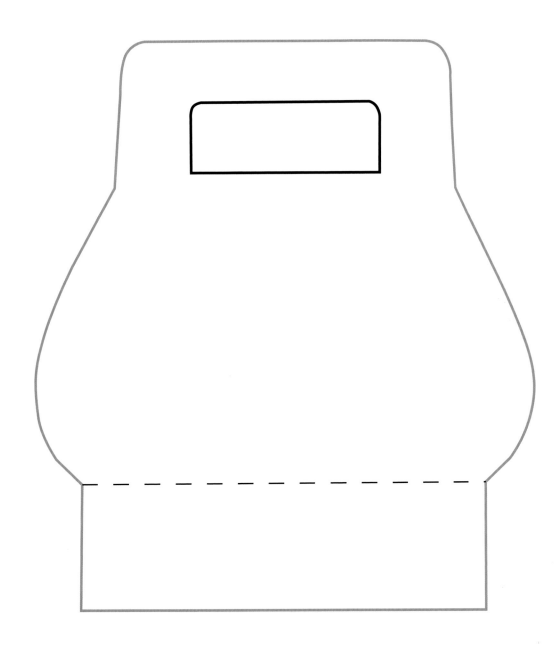

# Templates (cont.)

## Rice Bag Template

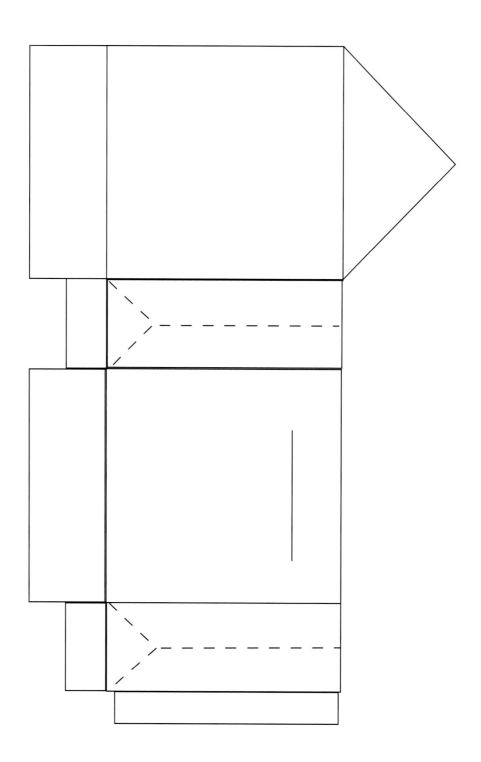

# Barbie Skirt Template

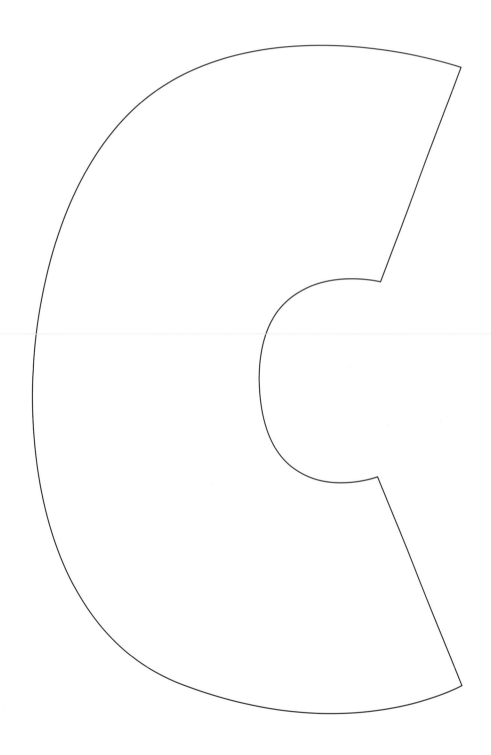

# Templates (cont.)

## Barbie Top Template

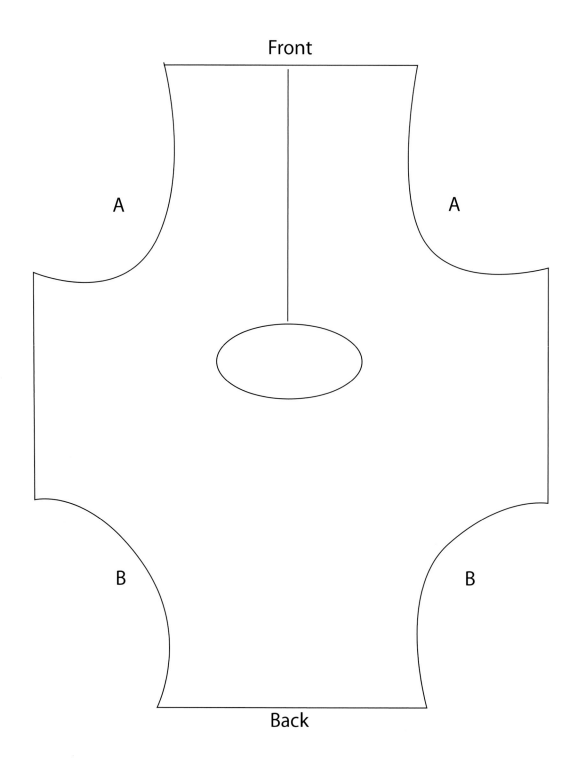

Front

A                    A

B                    B

Back

# Cut out Candy Box Template

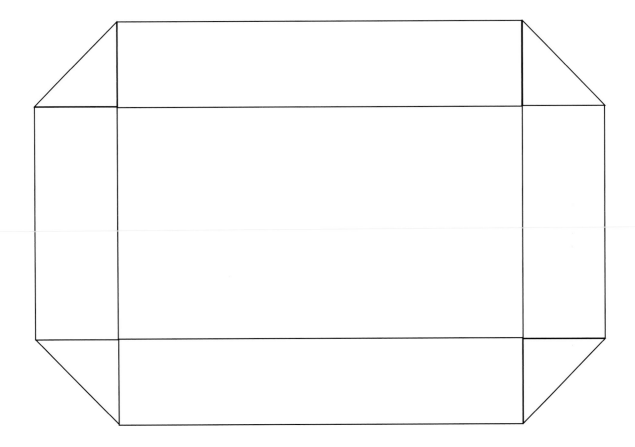

# Templates (cont.)

## Dreidel Favor Box Template

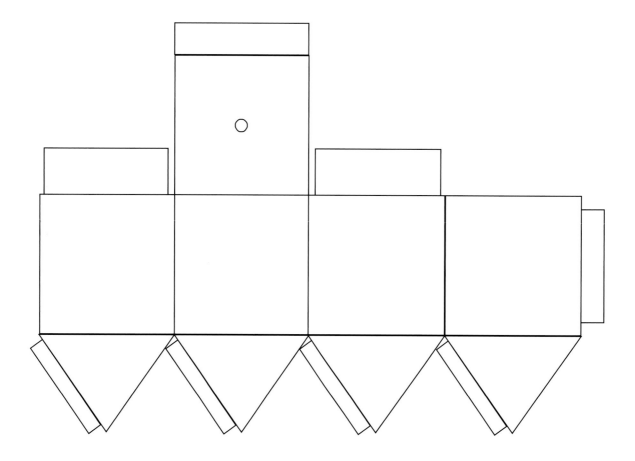

# Baby Blocks Favor Box Template

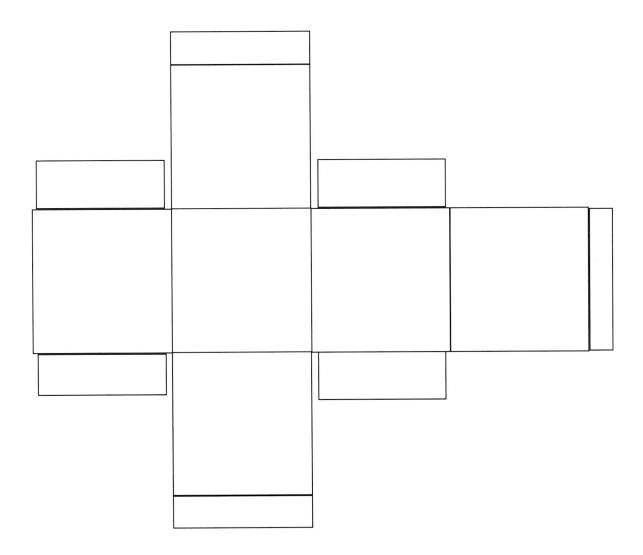

# Templates (cont.)

## Baby Bib Template

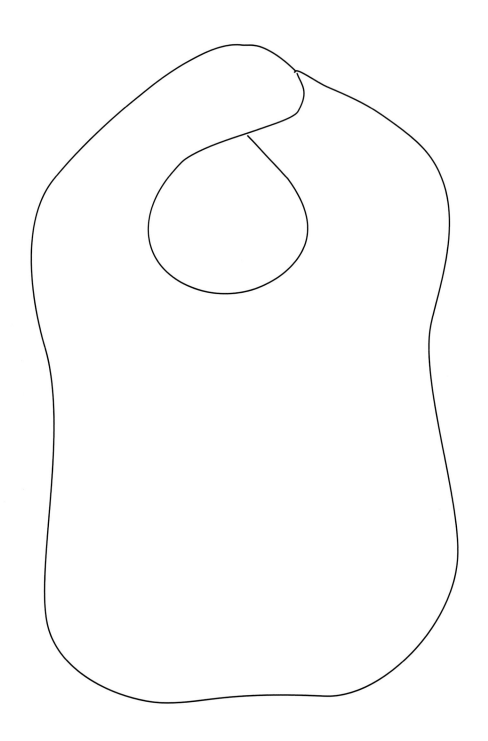

# Camera "Skin" Template

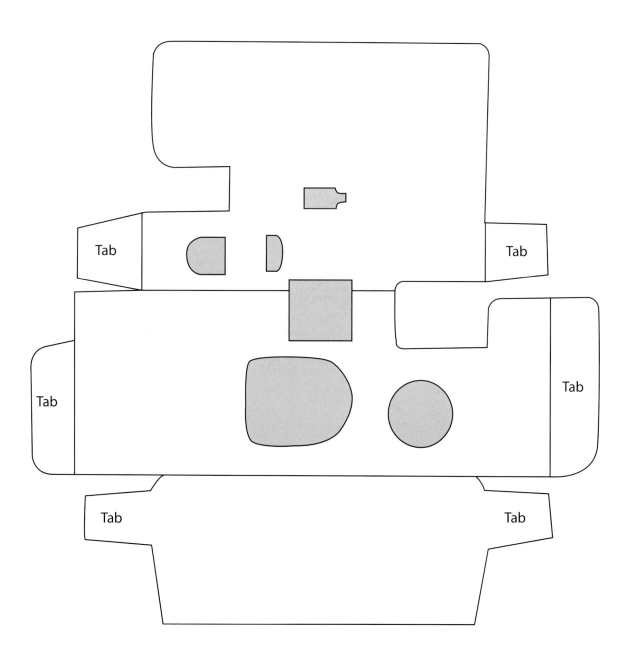

# Templates (cont.)

## Wedding Lights Template

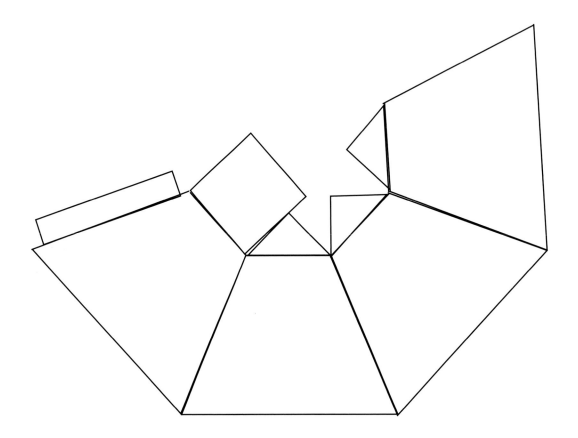

# Greeting Card Pop-up Piece Template

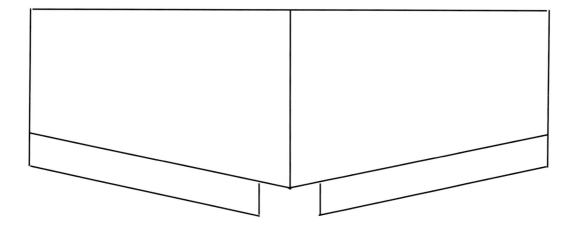

# Templates (cont.)

## Pop-up Sleeve Holiday Card Template

# Index

# Index (cont.)

textured, 31

transfer, *see* heat transfers

vellum, 29

types of inkjet compatible, 29

paper cutters and trimmers, 27-28

paper path, 22-23

photo editing, 13, 14

Photo Candle, 122, 122

Photo Display Plate, 87, 87

Photo Mug, Valentine, 90-91, 90

Photos in Glass Ornaments, 131, 131

photocopier, 19

PhotoFrost, 22

Photoshop (Adobe), 14, 25, 27

Photoshop Elements 3 (Adobe), 27

Piezoelectric printer (Epson), 19

pigment-based inks, 21-22

pillow, 25, 25

Place Cards, Pop-Up, 53-54, 53

Plate, Photo Display, 87, 87

Pop-Up Place Cards, 53-54, 53

Pop-Up Sleeve Holiday Card, 110-113, 110

Pop-Up, St. Patrick's Day Card, 125-126, 125

powder, embossing, 29, 31

Print Artist (Sierra), 25

lovers, 25

printable margins, 23

printers, *see* Alps MicroDry printers, bubble jet printers, inkjet printers, laser printers, *see also* individual brand names

print head, 19

PrintMaster (Broderbund), 11, 13, 25-26

Print Shop (Broderbund), 25

punches, paper, 27-28

Pyramid Box, Transparent, 132-133, 132

**R**

Rainbow Easter Basket, 92-93, 92

Revolving Musical Carousel, 94-96, 94

Purse Favor Bag, 62-64, 62

ribbons, printer, *see* Alps MicroDry printers

**S**

sales tax, 37

scanners and scanning, 24-25

scoring, 28

scrapbooking, 10

Scratch-Off Tickets, 103, 103

Self-Mailer, Vellum Insert, 127-128, 127

sealants, 27-28

Serif software, 25

setting, print

Shaker Card, St. Patrick's Day, 73-74, 73

shrink sheets, inkjet, 29

in stemware shrink charms, 64

spray starch, 59

software

freeware, 25

types available, 25-27

St. Patrick's Day Pop-Up Card, 125-126, 125

St. Patrick's Day Shaker Card, 73-74, 73

Stained Glass Votive Holder, 80, 80

starch, spray, 59

Stemware Shrink Charms, 65-66, 65

Sun Catcher, 79, 79

supplies, craft, *see* craft supplies

**T**

Table Tent, 106-107, 106

tape, removable, 27

templates, 45, *see also* Appendix C

Tickets, Scratch-off, 103, 103

tips and tricks, 31-32

toner, 19

toxicity, ink, 20-21

transfer blanks, heat, 30

translucent vellum, *see* Paper

Transparent Mini-Bag, 71-72, 71

Transparent Pyramid Box, 132-133 132

transparency, inkjet, *see* Film

T-shirts, 28

glitter embellished, 97, 97

**U**

ultraviolet light (UV) resistance, 21

unprintable area, 23

**V**

Valentine Photo Mug, 90-91, 90

vellum, *see also* paper

in fold-over invitation, 56

in insert self-mailer, 127-128

Vellum Insert Self-Mailer, 127-128, 127

vinyl, printable, *see* bumper sticker paper

Votive Candle Column, 108-109, 108

Votive Holder, Stained Glass, 80, 80

**W**

waterslip decals, 29, 30, 87

Wedding Lights, 129-130, 129

Wedding Heart Rice Bag, 67-68, 67

white, printing in, *see* Alps MicroDry printers

White Waterproof Window Cling, 117, 117

window cling, 29-30, 117

Windows operating system, 25, 31

World Wide Web, 13, *see also* Appendix A

message boards, 13

forums, 13

sites of interest, 13

**Y**

Yahoo Small Business, 40

**Z**

Z-hinge (Canon), 24